Other PC World Books

Getting Started with the IBM PC and XT
by David Arnold and the Editors of PC World

How to Buy an IBM PC or Compatible Computer
by Danny Goodman and the Editors of PC World

Essential Applications for the IBM PC and XT

Patrick Plemmons
and the Editors of PC World

PC World Books
Published by
Computer Book Division
Simon & Schuster, Inc.
New York

Published by the Computer Book Division
Simon & Schuster, Inc.
Simon & Schuster Building
Rockefeller Center
1230 Avenue of the Americas
New York, New York 10020

Manufactured in the United States of America

10 9 8 7 6 5 4 3 2 1

Library of Congress Cataloging in Publication Data

Plemmons, Patrick.
Essential applications for the IBM PC and XT.

Includes index.
1. IBM Personal Computer—Programming.
2. IBM Personal Computer XT—Programming.
I. PC World. II. Title. III. Title: Essential
applications for the I.B.M. P.C. and X.T.
QA76.8.I2594P49 1984 001.64'2 84-10697

ISBN 0-671-49279-9

Contents

Preface

The IBM PC and the XT have become industry standards in the world of business computers. Because of the preeminence of the PC, software authors have made the PC their choice for writing productivity programs. Thus, PC owners can choose from the widest array of first-class applications software available for personal computers.

But the flood of software for the PC has caused a problem, too. How can newcomers to computing know all the principal types of software for the PC, and how can they evaluate individual programs within each category? This book will help you tackle these difficult tasks.

This book is especially useful if you are just beginning to use a PC. Perhaps you are considering buying a PC and want to learn more about what it can really do for your business. Or you might be using your PC already for word processing or spreadsheets, and you want to add new applications. This book will introduce you to the full range of major business applications for the PC and will explain each application in depth—how each one works, and what features you should look for.

Providing information is the purpose of this book. It will expand your computing horizons by making you aware of the valuable and practical ways you can use the PC, and it will help you choose the appropriate applications programs to enhance your productivity.

I want to thank the people at PC World Books who contributed to this volume, especially Jeremy Joan Hewes, who conceived of and edited the book, and Betsy Dilernia and Lindy Wankoff, who managed the production process.

Essential Applications for the IBM PC and XT

INTRODUCTION

Software for Increasing Productivity

The IBM PC and XT are two of the most versatile and useful personal computers on the market today. But many of the people who use personal computers for one part of their work are unaware of the numerous other business applications available to them. As a result, they tap only a small part of their computer's power.

This book introduces you to the rich variety of applications software for the IBM PC and compatible computers. It is intended for business people and others who are already using a PC or an XT but want to do more with it. Because we assume that you are familiar with the PC and how it works, we concentrate on the applications themselves.

Six major software categories are presented. Five are single applications for desktop computers—spreadsheets, word processing, data base management, business graphics, and accounting—and the sixth is integrated programs. Each category has two chapters devoted to it. The first chapter in each pair introduces the application, discusses the features that programs in that category should have to make them useful tools, and suggests tasks for which you can use the software.

Each major application has a second chapter that introduces two or three popular programs in that category. The chapters cover the program's features, documentation, uses, and manufacturer support. You may find that one or more of these programs are suited to your particular business needs; if not, the discussions will provide criteria for choosing among the many other available programs.

Chapter 1 provides an overview of the six applications, and Chapter 14 briefly covers some other important applications, including communications, project management, and time management.

CHAPTER ONE

An Overview of Applications

The advances in microcomputers during recent years have been astounding, but equally noteworthy are the advances that have been made in personal computer software—the programs that make the computer run. Without these programs, the flashy new hardware would be useless.

Software has come a long way during the past year or so, and an important factor in software improvement was the success of the IBM PC. As the PC and compatible computers captured more and more of the market for personal computers, software companies responded by creating thousands of new programs that take advantage of the features of these machines. Such a wealth of good programs now exists for the PC and the XT that IBM compatibility has become an industry standard.

Increased Memory and Improved Programs

The first commercially viable personal computer for business and personal productivity, the Apple II, was based on an 8-bit microprocessor (also called the central processing unit, or CPU). An 8-bit microprocessor handles data in groups of 8 bits at a time, but more importantly, it can address only 64K of random-access memory (RAM), approximately 64,000 characters—bytes—of data. RAM, or internal memory, is where the computer keeps data that it is working on, including programs.

But productivity software that is both powerful and easy to use often requires a lot of internal memory. For example, some data base management programs and integrated programs discussed in later chapters require up to 256K of RAM, far beyond the capacity of earlier 8-bit personal computer systems.

Personal computers, such as the PC, that are based on 16-bit microprocessors, can theoretically address up to 1 megabyte (1 million bytes) of memory and can therefore support larger and more sophisticated software than 8-bit computers. The PC comes with 64K of RAM, which can be expanded to a maximum of 640K by adding expansion boards. The XT comes with 128K of RAM, which can be expanded to 640K. In addition to their substantially larger memory capacities, 16-bit computer systems process data faster than 8-bit systems, especially numerical data. PC-standard computers cleared the way for the development of large, sophisticated programs.

The PC and the XT

The PC's flexible, modular design has set the standard by which contemporary personal computer systems are judged. The typical PC consists of a System Unit, which houses the CPU, power source, floppy disk drives, input/output connections, and adapter boards; a detached keyboard that has function keys and a numeric keypad; and a high-resolution monitor, either monochrome or color, that displays 80 columns and 25 lines, with uppercase and lowercase text.

With an optional color graphics board and a color monitor, the PC can display full-color business graphics. The PC also supports a broad range of the most popular dot matrix and letter quality printers, graphics plotters, and modems for communicating with other computers. Multifunction memory boards are available from independent manufacturers to expand the PC's internal memory to its maximum, 640K.

The XT is an extended version of the PC that has more memory and more storage capacity in its standard configuration than the PC. Whereas the PC uses one or two floppy disk drives to store data, the XT has one floppy disk drive and a 10-megabyte hard disk. The hard disk enables you to store and rapidly access a considerably larger amount of data than the PC, whose floppy disks hold up to 360K of data each. The hard, or fixed, disk in the XT is built into the System Unit and occupies the same amount of space as a floppy drive. The hard disk enables the computer to handle tasks that require manipulating large amounts of stored data, as is common in data base management and accounting. Although a 10-megabyte hard disk can hold up to 5000 typewritten pages of data, many business applications can quickly use up that amount of storage.

The XT's internal memory capacity ranges from the standard 128K to a maximum of 640K. The standard XT also comes with a serial communications port for attaching a modem or another peripheral device. It features eight expansion slots (the PC provides only five) in the System Unit, where circuit boards can be inserted to add features such as color graphics, an internal modem, or additional memory. Three of the slots are initially filled at the factory, leaving five slots for further expansion. IBM also offers an Expansion Unit for the PC that upgrades it to the XT configuration.

The IBM PC and XT have formidable capabilities for carrying out business applications. The 16-bit microprocessor can efficiently handle large and complex spreadsheets, and the large internal memory capacities enable users to run large, sophisticated programs. The PC's high-resolution Monochrome Display and its excellent keyboard make it ideal for word processing. And both the PC and the XT can produce sophisticated business graphics using a graphics-capable monochrome or color monitor and the appropriate adapter.

You can tailor a system to fit your specific requirements and integrate any advances in hardware or software into an IBM desktop system, as needed. (The PC World Book entitled *How to Buy an IBM PC or Compatible Computer* will help you select the components for your system.) Best of all, however, is the PC's tremendous and still-growing library of business and productivity software. Applications for the PC range from simple mailing list programs to sophisticated decision-making tools and information-retrieval systems that can provide executives with up-to-the-minute business information.

The PC excels in applications software, and its operating system, PC-DOS, is fast becoming an industry standard. PC-DOS is the PC and XT version of MS-DOS (Microsoft), and the two operating systems are almost identical. What this means for you is that independent software publishers are actively writing software that is compatible with MS-DOS and PC-DOS, assuring an expanding array of excellent business software for the PC and compatible computers.

Applications Software

There are two types of software for the PC: system and applications. System software, such as PC-DOS, makes up the computer's operating system and functions as the manager for the system. The disk operating system (DOS) controls the basic functions of the computer, such as data input and output, and enables you to run applications programs.

Applications programs are generally more meaningful than system software to most users interested in increasing their productivity with personal computers. An applications program enables you to perform a specific task, such as posting data to a general ledger, while the operating system works in the background, requiring minimal attention and faithfully managing the computer's functions. Applications programs perform all the major business tasks, including writing, filing, calculating, and transmitting electronic data.

Although applications programs have different purposes, they all have common elements. The program itself is provided on one or more floppy disks. With the program disk comes documentation (often referred to as the user manual), and occasionally a tutorial to help the user learn the program. Some tutorials are meant to be read, while others teach you to use the program while sitting at the computer. The best tutorials "interact" with the user; they make you practice as a means of helping you learn the program. Some programs provide both written and interactive tutorials.

Unfortunately, documentation is often poorly executed. When first learning a program, you are highly dependent on the documentation to explain and demonstrate program use. Excellent programs can seem difficult to learn if the manuals are overly technical or confusing. Luckily, there is presently a thriving business in supplemental books and instructional materials for popular applications programs.

Although each kind of applications program has a different kind of task to accomplish, all programs use screens to create a visual format, usually called the *interface,* where you can enter, manipulate, and transfer data. Word processing programs, for example, have editing screens where text is typed; spreadsheets use screens designed for columns and rows of figures; and data base management programs have data entry screens. These screens typically have borders and rulers to define the program's work area. Screens that are logically organized and comprehensible go a long way toward making a program easy to use.

Most programs use the cursor to define the location where an operation is to take place. Although the cursor has different shapes in different programs, most often it is a small blinking character that the user positions on screen where information is to be entered or changed. The cursor may be controlled by the keyboard or by a pointing device called a mouse, a small hand-held electronic device that moves the cursor on the screen as you move it over a flat surface, such as a desktop. Many people consider the mouse to be easier and faster for moving the cursor around the screen than cursor keys or key combinations.

The user tells a program what to do by typing commands or selecting options presented in on-screen menus. Commands are instructions given to the computer to make it perform certain functions, such as printing or editing. Command-driven programs require the user to learn and remember a series of keystrokes to direct operations. Although such programs are sometimes difficult to learn, they are flexible in the functions they perform. *WordStar* (MicroPro International Corporation), one of the most popular word processing programs, is largely command-driven. To save a document with *WordStar,* for example, you hold down the <Ctrl> key while typing KD. Because KD is not mnemonically related to "saving" a file, many people consider this type of command difficult to learn. Many programs use mnemonic commands, such as "S" for "Save," which are far easier to remember than *WordStar*'s more esoteric commands.

Other programs organize related commands into groups known as menus. Program menus are displayed on the screen and offer clear choices throughout the program. Although menu-driven programs are usually easy to learn because all the information is right in front of you, having to read through a series of menus even after you have learned a program is generally a nuisance. (Some programs do, however, enable you to control just how much "help" you want displayed on the screen.)

Another common element in applications programs, especially menu-driven programs, is screen prompts. A prompt is an on-screen message that tells you what to do next or asks you to confirm a command that you have entered. For instance, when you try to erase an entire spreadsheet, most spreadsheet programs have a prompt that asks you to confirm whether you mean to delete the entire spreadsheet. Extensive use of prompts makes programs easy to follow, but again, once you have mastered a program, you might find prompts irritating.

A file storage system is also a common element of applications programs. Although the procedural steps involved in saving and loading information to and from disks vary from program to program, the essential concepts are almost identical. You use commands or menu selections provided by the applications program for file handling. When information is saved on the disk, it is recorded there with an identifying file name. Most often, you are asked to choose a name that should help you remember the contents of the file. Once a file is safely stored on disk, you can reload it into memory any time you want to access it.

Information isn't much good unless you can print it on paper. Almost all applications programs provide some means of printing information as reports, letters, word processing documents, or even charts and graphs. Data is printed by sending information created by the computer over a cable to a printer. The printer reads the incoming signals and prints the pages according to the layout specified by the instructions from the computer.

Applications programs usually allow you to use commands or menus to choose the way a document should print. Unfortunately, different applications programs use different instructions for printing. And because each printer requires a special set of instructions, you'll have to spend some time learning your applications program and your printer's capabilities to get them to work well together.

Spreadsheet Programs

The most popular application for the PC is undoubtedly the electronic spreadsheet. To understand what an electronic spreadsheet is and how it works, you have to understand a manual spreadsheet.

A manual spreadsheet is a paper worksheet arranged in columns and rows, the familiar matrix or ledger organization. Manual spreadsheets have long been used to analyze numerous financial applications, particularly accounting, budgeting, and pro forma financials. Typically, classes or categories of figures are entered as rows on the spreadsheet, while time periods or other goods are shown as columns. For instance, if a five-year budget for a business were written on a spreadsheet, each budget item would be entered in a different row, and each column would represent entries pertaining to a specific year. To find any item for any year, you would look at the intersection of a particular row item and column year. A key feature of spreadsheets is that data in one column often affects the data in other columns. If you make a change in one column, the figures in other dependent columns also change. Recalculating a large spreadsheet manually is a difficult and time-consuming task.

If you have worked with complex manual spreadsheets, you can appreciate the power and the elegance of an electronic spreadsheet. The electronic spreadsheet recreates the column-and-row format on your computer screen. An electronic spreadsheet typically has at least 63 columns and 254 rows; the columns are labeled with letters, and the rows have identifying numbers. The intersection of a column and a row—A2, for example—is called a *cell.* By positioning the cursor in the desired cell, you can write four types of information into a cell: numbers, text and labels, formulas, and functions.

Typing numbers and text while setting up an electronic spreadsheet is almost identical to filling in a manual spreadsheet. You organize the information you want in columns and rows, and then type in the figures and titles of each row and column on the screen, just as you would enter them by hand on paper.

The great advantage of the electronic spreadsheet is that the numbers you store in the individual cells can be used to calculate and automatically display related numbers in other cells. Such calculations are accomplished by the storage of mathematical formulas in specific cells.

Formulas enable you to create mathematical relationships among cells. For instance, you might specify that the contents of cell A6 would equal cell A1 minus cell A2. Regardless of the actual numbers in cells A1 and A2, you would always get the desired result in cell A6.

This ability to define abstract mathematical relationships among cells—called *modeling*—is the key to the spreadsheet's power and utility. An electronic spreadsheet becomes a structure of mathematically related cells. You plug in the basic data or the assumptions, and the spreadsheet computes the rest. And once you create the initial spreadsheet model, or template, for a yearly income statement, for example, you can use it year after year and simply substitute each new year's figures.

Functions are frequently used formulas, such as net present value or internal rate of return, that the spreadsheet automatically enters and computes. Most spreadsheets also have powerful commands that simplify prolonged mathematical calculations. Once you have constructed your spreadsheet model using these functions and commands and have entered all your data, the spreadsheet automatically calculates the entire model. You can then change some of the figures and recalculate the whole model again, almost instantly. Let's say that you have constructed a pro forma investment analysis based on financing at 10 percent. Later you discover that the interest rate has jumped to 12 percent. Simply replace 10 percent with 12 percent in your spreadsheet model, and the program will automatically recalculate the entire spreadsheet.

There are so many uses for spreadsheets that it would be difficult to list them all. Some of the more common uses include pro forma financials, budgets, bids, sales forecasts, accounting, investment evaluation, tax planning, lease versus buy, and business plans. But that's just the beginning of a very long list. Spreadsheets are so versatile that they have literally innumerable applications.

Word Processing

Word processing is a major improvement over the old manual typewriter. Not only will a word processing program enable you to type text and edit it electronically, but you can also change page format during or after initial typing and print letter-perfect copy. You are free to add, delete, or revise lines of text, rearrange text, and create page layouts according to whatever dimensions are required, until you get them just right. After that, you can print the document as many times as you like, at speeds much faster than you could ever hope to type. And even then, you can still automatically change the text minutes, days, or months later, if needed, and easily print it again. Word processing is such a useful application that many people use the PC for that function alone.

A word processing program performs three basic functions: editing, formatting, and printing. The key element in editing is the edit screen, where you enter, edit, and view text. The formatting function offers an array of features that enable you to determine how the finished copy will appear on paper. The printing function enables you to direct the printer to produce different types and styles of printing.

During editing, you can insert or delete letters, words, or whole blocks of text. After any of these operations, most programs automatically reformat text to accommodate changes. You can also move text to new positions within a document or have the program search for a certain word or phrase and replace it with another word or phrase every time it appears. Some programs display text on the screen exactly as it will print on paper; other programs require you to insert formatting codes in a document that provide specific instructions to the printer.

Word processing not only lets you produce documents more efficiently, it also provides text-processing operations that are impossible to perform with a typewriter. Depending on its features, a program may be able to create indexes, footnotes, or a table of contents for documents that you produce. Some programs provide a spelling checker that can proofread a document and correct misspelled words, or a print merge feature that allows you to print personalized form letters without having to type the letter more than once. Features such as automatic page numbering and the ability to print repetitive text, or headers and footers, at the top and the bottom of every page are now standard in most word processing programs.

Virtually anything that you type on a typewriter can be done faster and better with a word processor. Whether you use it for business correspondence, long reports, speeches, press releases, book manuscripts, or short memos, word processing is certain to add power and efficiency to your writing.

Data Base Management Systems

A data base management system (DBMS) is a tool for storing information in a systematic order, so that you can retrieve all or part of the information when you need it. A dictionary is a simple manual data base manager system, as is an office filing system. Each provides systematic organization and access to specific information. Although an electronic data base manager is a similar tool, it provides faster information access and greater manipulative power in how that information is arranged than any paper system.

Unlike a word processing program, a DBMS is highly structured and requires that data be entered in a precise format. Many DBMS programs are complicated and difficult to learn, especially for novices. But an electronic DBMS is usually so much better than a paper filing system that learning it is usually worth the effort. The promise of replacing a multitude of manila folders with a few thin disks should be incentive enough for mastering a DBMS.

There are three categories of DBMSs generally supported by the PC: file manager, relational DBMS, and network or hierarchical DBMS. Although a file management system is the most basic DBMS, some are quite sophisticated. With a file manager, you can set up a single file, such as a list of buyers for one of your products, enter a variety of information about each buyer, and then use the program to access information about particular buyers and print reports when needed. A relational DBMS is more powerful than a file manager, but it requires you to learn some new tricks. A relational DBMS can operate on multiple files and provides flexibility in designing and modifying the organization of your data base. The network or hierarchical DBMS is highly demanding in terms of planning and structuring a data base and is generally inflexible if you later need to change it. But this type of system is fast, efficient, and powerful. For most users, even business users, a file manager or a relational DBMS is usually more than adequate for managing data.

Before you build a data base of information, you must know the types and the amount of information that will be stored in it. What specific information will be recorded, and what subcategories of information must also be included? What central item of information will most easily enable you to find what you're looking for? For example, will you organize your data around a customer's last name or an account number?

You must generally determine the types of information you will need from the data base and make sure that information is included and easily accessible. When you have decided on the data base structure, it's time to enter the data. Most programs lead you through data entry with screens that you complete in a "fill-in-the-blanks" manner. Once your data base is recorded on the PC, you can access and manipulate the information using the commands in the DBMS program. Finally, you can generate and print a variety of reports.

For business users, data management is especially useful in accounting, and personnel departments make great use of data base programs for managing and updating employee records. Marketing departments do computerized market research using such programs. Investment analysis, inventory, invoicing, and customer relations are all examples of organized systems of information that a DBMS can handle well.

Business Graphics

Business graphics is one of the most easily understood applications for the PC. Business graphics programs create charts and graphs of all kinds, in color or in black and white.

Because most business graphics programs are run by making selections from menus, they tend to be easy to use, but sometimes the quality of the charts they produce doesn't measure up to more sophisticated standards set by professional graphic artists. Still, the speed and the cost-effectiveness of these programs in producing visual aids make them valuable in today's businesses. A well-executed chart can add life to a business presentation and make points dramatically and succinctly.

Good business graphics programs can produce at least five basic types of business charts: area, bar, line, pie, and point. The better programs produce variations on these basic kinds of charts, such as exploded pie charts or three-dimensional bar charts. These programs offer flexibility in formatting a chart with different types of line styles, shading, labels, and legends. Some programs enable you to create different types of charts on the screen for comparison before printing. Because most graphics programs can also convert the output from other programs, such as spreadsheets, into graphics, you don't even have to reenter data to create a chart. Sophisticated business graphics programs, such as *VisiTrend/Plot* (VisiCorp), even incorporate time series analysis such as linear regression.

Graphics programs have three basic functions: formatting, data entry, and output. Formatting consists of choosing the type of graph you want and defining labels, colors, and textures. With programs that use templates to automate the formatting process, you fill in the blanks to structure a chart. Data is entered by the use of menus and prompts, and the program produces a perfectly scaled chart. When you're satisfied with the chart's appearance, you can print it on paper using a dot matrix printer or a graphics plotter.

You can also use these programs to prepare transparencies for presentation. Although business graphics software may not always produce work that has the quality of a professional artist, it is fast and relatively inexpensive.

Integrated Applications

Integrated programs are designed to complement the way business people really work—they allow you to perform several business functions simultaneously. By combining applications such as word processing, spreadsheets, and graphics, integrated programs enable you to move from one function to another in the natural course of working on a project.

Some confusion exists about what integration means. At the most basic level, programs within the same product line that can exchange information are integrated. These product "families" include the *pfs:* programs from Software Publishing Corporation and the series of programs in *WordStar Professional* from MicroPro International Corporation.

All-in-one programs that combine several applications on one disk constitute the next level of integration. *1-2-3* (Lotus Development Corporation) and *MBA* (Context Management Systems) are two of the best known all-in-one programs. They provide spreadsheet, data base, graphics, and other functions in a set of integrated components.

Yet another type of integration is provided by operating environments such as *Visi On* (VisiCorp), *Microsoft Windows* (Microsoft), and *DesQ* (Quarterdeck Office Systems). Using an operating environment, you can choose which applications to link and then manipulate the resulting data with sophisticated systems of screen windows, icons, or perhaps a mouse for cursor movement.

A common combination of applications is spreadsheet and business graphics. Data base management and word processing are two other core functions of integrated programs. Some integrated programs have a central application around which other applications cluster. For example, *1-2-3* centers on an especially powerful spreadsheet.

Program families achieve integration by recording information in a common format that can be read by the other related programs. You can run one application, create the files you want, store them on disk, and then run another program to manipulate the data.

All-in-one programs offer a high degree of integration. Using either the keyboard or a mouse, you can move directly among the various applications simply by entering commands. Because you don't have to switch program disks, your time can be used efficiently. But the trade-off for the joys of all-in-one integration is that some of the programs are very slow.

Operating environments are fast and powerful. The programs enable you to move quickly from one application to another, or work with more than one application at a time.

Accounting Programs

Accounting software helps maintain the financial records of a business. Large businesses have had interactive, automated accounting systems for years, but now scaled down versions of these systems are available for small and medium-sized businesses, thanks to the power and affordability of PC-standard computers.

Accounting programs can perform all the major elements in an integrated accounting system. They can handle the functions of general ledger, accounts receivable, accounts payable, inventory, payroll, sales invoicing, and job costing. Most accounting software is modular; you can buy the core applications such as general ledger, accounts receivable, and accounts payable, and then add other modules as you need them.

The capabilities of accounting programs vary greatly from program to program. Some programs process relatively small amounts of information, while more elaborate systems have sophisticated features and prodigious capacities. Because of the size of some of these larger accounting systems (one program for the PC uses 16 disks), it's almost mandatory that you run them on an XT or a PC that has a hard disk.

Data is entered into an accounting program through formatted screens. Once the data has been processed, the program generates a variety of accounting reports, such as income statements, balance sheets, and invoices. Better programs offer sophisticated report writers that enable you to design reports to fit your particular needs.

Although the primary purpose of accounting software is to maintain an accounting system, these programs generate a tremendous amount of data that can be used for other important business functions, such as budgeting, forecasting, marketing, tax planning, and investment analysis. Information that is generated by accounting programs can sometimes be used by other applications programs such as *1-2-3* or *dBASE II* (Ashton-Tate).

Other Business Applications

Although the six major applications just discussed are the best known and most widely used, there are several other useful and popular applications for PC-standard computers. One is communications, which enables you to exchange information between your PC and other computers, including mainframe computers that have vast data bases. Other programs handle project management, including costing, scheduling, and critical path analysis. *TK!Solver* (Software Arts) is an equation processor that is ideal for professions, such as engineering, in which complex formulas must be solved routinely. Another common business application is time management.

Personal computers are rapidly becoming the de facto executive work stations in integrated business information networks. As valuable as your PC is for stand-alone applications, it can be even more valuable if it works with other computers. Using a modem, you can communicate over the telephone lines with other computers and exchange information. Communications software controls that information exchange. In a large business, you might connect with the company's mainframe and work with the information that it provides. A small business or personal user might access data from the many on-line commercial data bases to vastly expand information resources.

Project management programs enable you to plan and control complicated projects, meet deadlines even when critical project parameters change, and manage costs in great detail. These programs automatically calculate the critical path for your project and display the sequence of steps that most efficiently complete the job. If a major factor of the project changes, such as a deadline, the program automatically revises schedules and costs accordingly.

At present, *TK!Solver* is a unique application. Billed as an equation processor, it has the ability to interpret and solve mathematical expressions as equations. You can also use *TK!Solver* to convert units of measurement, create charts, and make tables. It virtually eliminates most of the painstaking effort of solving common polynomial equations, and makes solving complex algebraic equations a snap.

Anyone who juggles a complicated and fast-changing personal schedule every day will appreciate time management software. These programs schedule your daily activities, file and recall information relating to your schedule, and print out memos or lists to help you get organized. Rather than relying on scribbled notes, hasty referrals to illegible calendar markings, or a secretary to coordinate meetings that go on interminably, time management software offers an easy way to organize and schedule business activities.

As you can see, many effective and time-saving applications programs are available to reduce the complexity and weight of your workload. Whether the main thrust of your work is accounting, project tracking, or writing elegant business correspondence, the PC and the XT provide an exemplary means of doing it quickly and well. And the many applications presented here will add power and versatility to your work with the computer.

CHAPTER TWO

Spreadsheets

The electronic spreadsheet was the first major business application developed for the personal computer, and it remains the most popular. The first electronic spreadsheet, *VisiCalc* (VisiCorp), was released on January 1, 1979, for use with the Apple II personal computer, and it's no exaggeration to say that *VisiCalc* created the business market for the personal computer.

VisiCalc was a breakthrough product, because it could be applied to many common business activities. The program gave managers and professionals the freedom to solve complex computational problems without the restrictions on time and resources often imposed by corporate data processing departments. The response to *VisiCalc* was nothing short of extraordinary, and this initial success spawned a wave of imitators.

Spreadsheets have evolved considerably since *VisiCalc*'s introduction five years ago. Just as the development of the personal computer itself made a program like *VisiCalc* possible, enhancements to personal computer hardware have enabled spreadsheet developers to add many powerful and efficient features to electronic spreadsheets.

The development of powerful new microprocessors that can address large amounts of internal memory, and the corresponding development of affordable memory chips to provide that larger internal memory, have given spreadsheet developers the raw material to make their products bigger, faster, and more functional. With its fast and powerful 16-bit microprocessor, capacious internal memory, good keyboard, and ample data storage capacity, the IBM PC is ideal for spreadsheet applications.

First-generation spreadsheets, such as *VisiCalc* (VisiCorp), *SuperCalc* (Sorcim/IUS Micro Software), and *CalcStar* (MicroPro), had all the basic functions of today's spreadsheets, but none of the bells and whistles. Early spreadsheets had the relatively limited capacity of 63 columns and 254 rows, while *1-2-3* (Lotus Development), one of today's largest spreadsheets, has a capacity of 256 columns and 2048 rows. And *1-2-3* integrates graphics and limited data base management capabilities with the spreadsheet.

Defining Spreadsheets

As noted briefly in Chapter 1, a spreadsheet organizes data in the familiar matrix of vertical columns and horizontal rows (see Figure 2.1). (Both the program and the models it produces are often collectively known as spreadsheets. To avoid confusion, this book refers to the program as a spreadsheet and to the program's product as a *worksheet*.) Rows usually hold classes of data, and columns typically represent time periods. Individual entries are related to one another mathematically. A simple worksheet might calculate the gross margin on the sale of a product. You could have three rows, designating sales price, cost of goods sold, and gross margin. For any given year, represented by a column, the gross margin equals the sales price minus the cost of goods sold. (This is, of course, a very simple example.) With a spreadsheet program, you can build and solve extremely complex problems using the ledger-style method of organization and computation.

Whether limited or loaded with options, all spreadsheet programs work the same way. Before you even turn on the computer, you should plan your worksheet layout. Good planning saves time and yields better results than trying to design a worksheet as you go along. Next, you build the worksheet

B4 (V) +B1−B2 C
268

	A	B	C	D	E	F	G	H
1		January	February	March	April	May	June	July
2	Sales	100	200	100	400			
3	Cost	60	120	60	240			
4	NET	40	80	40	160			
5								
6								
7								
8								
9								
10								
11								
12								
13								
14								
15								
16								
17								
18								
19								
20								
21								

Figure 2.1 *The ledger-style screen of* VisiCalc, *the first electronic spreadsheet.*

on the screen; this is where most of the work takes place. To build an electronic worksheet, you enter labels and headings, formulas, and functions by invoking commands built into the program. Once your worksheet is structured to your satisfaction, you enter the necessary data and command the program to calculate the results; if necessary, you make adjustments and have the program recalculate.

Spreadsheet programs are useful because they are not limited to processing one set of data—rather, they are models that can be used repeatedly. The user can substitute new data and keep some or all of the formulas used for calculations. For example, once you have constructed a worksheet to calculate your income taxes, that same worksheet can do your taxes year after year; all you have to do is enter the new data. When tax laws and regulations change, you can update the formulas, functions, and tables in the worksheet model to reflect the changes. This modeling capability enables the skilled spreadsheet user to create templates (reusable models) that can in turn be employed by people who have little knowledge of the program—or, for that matter, little experience with personal computers at all.

Forecasting is a critical success factor for any business. Although planning months or years in advance is essential, given the pace of change in today's world, it is almost impossible to predict variables such as interest rates and inflation. The best most businesses can do is develop a range of estimates for any given occurrence. Such hypothetical analyses are natural applications for the electronic spreadsheet, because it has the ability to recalculate large arrays of numbers easily.

For example, assume you're doing a break-even analysis for the introduction of a new product. You've priced the product at $1, and you need to capture 10 percent of the market each year to break even in three years. What would the effect be if you charged 50 cents for your product? Or $1.50? And what if you can capture only 5 percent of the market the first year? This type of analysis is an ideal application for spreadsheets. You simply change the price or market percentage recorded in the sheet, and the program recalculates the entire model and immediately shows the new results.

Although you can obviously work faster with an electronic spreadsheet than on paper, you should also be able to work better, because you have more freedom to experiment and analyze your models. But anyone who has worked with forecasting knows that the results of the model are only as good as the assumptions put into it. The spreadsheet is a tool—not a solution.

Common Spreadsheet Features

To get the most from any tool, you have to know how to use it. This is especially true for spreadsheets. Although someone new to personal computing can use spreadsheets effectively after only a few hours of practice, using a spreadsheet program efficiently for complicated jobs requires many hours of experience and an in-depth understanding of the program's features. Many of the enhancements of the latest spreadsheets that are especially useful for specific applications may be overlooked or ignored by less knowledgeable users.

Although different spreadsheet programs use slightly different terminology and operating procedures, the basic features are the same. For purposes of illustration, we use *VisiCalc* terminology, because it's the model on which most other spreadsheets are based.

As noted previously, the worksheet appears on the screen as a matrix of columns and rows. Columns are labeled with letters, and rows are numbered. The intersections of columns and rows are called cells, and cells are referenced by their column and row coordinates. Cell A1 is the cell in the upper left corner of the worksheet, A2 is directly below it, and cell B1 is directly to its right.

There are several ways to view different parts of a worksheet. Because the screen usually displays a limited portion of a worksheet, you can scroll through the rows and the columns vertically and horizontally using the cursor movement keys. In most programs, the <Home> key automatically moves the cursor to the upper left corner of the worksheet. An especially useful command for cursor movement is Goto, which enables you to move the cursor directly to any cell in the spreadsheet.

Building a worksheet is a process of moving the cursor to various cells and entering text or data; the cell where the cursor is located is usually called the active cell. You can enter several types of information in cells: labels, in either text or numerical form; numbers; or formulas and functions. Labels are used to identify the rows and the columns of data, since an unlabeled column of numbers can be puzzling to someone reading the spreadsheet and trying to guess its function. The numbers you enter, of course, are the raw material for the calculations you design a worksheet to perform.

But the real power of the spreadsheet program is derived from the mathematical formulas that can be entered in a worksheet. These formulas essentially tell the program to perform a mathematical operation on data stored in one or more cells and display the result in the designated cell. Because the program performs calculations only on those cells that contain data, you must identify which cells hold labels and which cells hold data and formulas.

The user differentiates between labels and numbers by the first character entered in the cell. If the first character is a letter, the program assumes that a label will be entered. If the first character is a number or a mathematical operator, the program assumes that the entry is a number to be included in the calculations. You can, however, use a number for a label by first entering a double quotation mark.

All spreadsheet programs enable you to construct formulas using four mathematical operators: the plus and minus signs, the asterisk for multiplication, and the slash for division. The elements, or variables, in each formula can be cell names, with the result that whatever figure presently appears in the indicated cell will be used in the formula. If the contents of a cell named in a formula change, the formula is recalculated and the new result is displayed. For example, the contents of cell Y5 might be a formula that reads Y5 = Y3/Y4. No matter what data is in cells Y3 and Y4, the spreadsheet will return a value in cell Y5 that is equal to Y3 divided by Y4. If the contents of either Y3 or Y4 change, a new value in Y5 is displayed. (If there is no data in cells Y3 and Y4, or non-numerical data is entered in either cell, the program will display an error message.)

Although simple formulas such as the one just shown are not difficult to create or understand, spreadsheets also enable you to compose fairly formidable-looking algebraic formulas. One formula can direct addition, subtraction, division, and multiplication involving many different cells simultaneously. But in creating formulas (in which one cell is divided by another and the result multiplied by a third cell, for example), you must keep track of the order of the mathematical operations, or the results may not be the ones you were looking for. Most spreadsheets enable you to control the order of mathematical operations by inserting parentheses around cells that are to be treated together.

For complicated formulas, you must be aware of the calculating sequence followed by the program itself. For instance, a program might calculate division and multiplication before addition and subtraction. Any values within parentheses, however, are calculated first; therefore, you would not get, for example, the same result from the formula A5 = A2 + A3 * A4 that you would get from A5 = (A2 + A3) * A4.

Functions are simply often-used formulas that the designers have included to make the program easy to use. Two of the more useful spreadsheet functions for business are net present value, a technique for expressing future values in terms of today's dollars, and SUM, a simple mathematical function that returns the sum of a group of cells. The variables in a spreadsheet function are known as arguments, and arguments are represented by cell coordinates. For instance, the function R15 = @SUM(R5...R14) adds up the contents of the cells from R5 to R14 and displays the answer in cell R15. (The @ sign signifies that a mathematical function is being used.) Basic spreadsheets have a variety of mathematical, trigonometric, and statistical functions that can be applied to engineering and other professions, as well as business tasks.

Although the original version of *VisiCalc* didn't have them, most current versions of spreadsheet programs have logical functions, also known as Boolean functions. Logical functions are used with arithmetic comparison operators to create conditional statements that, in effect, enable the program to make decisions when faced with variations in the values of data. These logical functions include "true," "false," "and," "or," "not," and "if." Some common arithmetic comparison operators are > for "greater than," < for "less than," and = for "equals." Logical functions enable you to create worksheets that can determine the commission a salesperson should receive if his or her monthly sales reach a certain level. The program can actually use the logical functions to look at the amount of sales and choose the commission rate that applies to the conditions stated in the data.

A logical function might look like the following: @IF(B10<B9,B8,B7). This is a typical IF...THEN...ELSE function. If the value in cell B10 (sales) is less than the one in B9 (the amount of sales necessary to qualify for the higher commission), then use the value that is in cell B8 (lower commission rate); if it is more, then use the value in cell B7 (higher commission rate). Logical functions are extremely useful features. They enable you to apply spreadsheets to complicated

tasks, such as calculating taxes, in which different actions are required depending on the value of many other variables, such as income level and number of deductions.

A basic spreadsheet program generally contains functions for elementary data management. Two such functions that get data from lists constructed within the spreadsheet are called Choose and Lookup. Choose allows you to select certain data from a list of choices, which can include the contents of different cells. Using the Choose function, you essentially set up the function to select a specific cell based on a key number. If you entered @CHOOSE(3,A1,A2,A3,A4,A5), for example, the value returned would always be A3. The first number in the sequence, 3, is the key, and the subsequent cell numbers comprise the list. In this example, if you had used 2 as the key or first number, the value returned would have been A2. The key in our example was a set number (2 or 3), but to get the full power of the Choose function you can use a key based on a cell's contents. The Choose function would then make various selections based on the figure entered in the key cell.

Lookup is a similar function, except that it uses an indexed table. You build the table in two contiguous rows or columns of the worksheet. Each entry in one row, designated as the search row, is the index for an item in the adjoining row (or column). The best example of the Lookup function, and the one for which it was developed, is income tax. Using this function, you could have the program calculate the proper tax rate by searching a list of incomes. These useful but simple data management functions are greatly enhanced in the newer spreadsheet programs.

Spreadsheet Commands

So far we have talked a lot about spreadsheet capabilities but little about how to put those capabilities to use. To create a worksheet, you use commands. Early spreadsheet programs have a basic set of commands used for formatting, entering data, calculating, and printing. Even though these commands differ slightly among programs, the basic commands usually follow *VisiCalc*'s conventions.

Many of the commands are used to format the worksheet. The Format command enables you to control the way data appears in a cell. Data can be displayed as an integer or a whole number, as dollars and cents, left or right justified, or displayed graphically as a series of horizontal asterisks. Depending on the type of data you are using, the Format command can make data entry much more efficient. For example, if one column of a worksheet will always contain sums of money, that column could be formatted to display the numbers as dollars and cents.

The Global command handles formatting chores for the entire worksheet. By invoking the Global command, you can set the format for every cell in the worksheet, using the same options that are available in the Format command. In the original version of *VisiCalc,* all the columns had to be the same width, so you had to use Global to change cell width. Change one, and you had to change them all. This significant formatting weakness has been rectified in later versions of *VisiCalc,* as well as in such other spreadsheets as *SuperCalc* and *Multiplan* (Microsoft).

Delete and Insert are two formatting commands that are sometimes called "cut-and-paste" commands. The Delete command removes a column or a row from the worksheet and reformats the sheet to accommodate the deletion. The Insert command inserts a blank column or row into the worksheet. Both commands offer flexibility in designing your worksheet, so that you can add or delete information when necessary.

VisiCalc provides a Move command to help you redesign the worksheet. This command moves a column or a row to a different location in the worksheet. Once you enter data, you can relocate it later, if necessary. The program automatically reformats the areas affected by the movement.

One command that can save you a lot of work building a spreadsheet is Replicate. This command enables you to duplicate the contents of a cell or group of cells without retyping them. Replicate is especially useful for formulas or functions that are repeated throughout a worksheet. If you wanted to total the contents of cells A1 through A6, for example, you would type the sum function, A7 = @SUM(A1...A6), in cell A7. If you also wanted to total the contents of a related column, such as B1 through B6 and C1 through C6, you could use the Replicate command to duplicate the A7 SUM function in cells B7 and C7. Replicate can keep you from having to fill cells repeatedly with the same numbers or formulas, and it automatically enters the correct row or column name (B7 instead of A7 in column B, for example).

VisiCalc, like many of its newer imitators, enables you to divide the screen into windows. A window is simply a subdivision of the display, a handy way to compare different parts of a worksheet. Within each window, a different part of the total worksheet can be viewed or operated on. The original version of *VisiCalc* offered two windows.

Because you can view only a limited portion of the worksheet at any time, sometimes you can't see the labels that signify the meaning of rows and columns of numbers. This can cause confusion as you examine the screen. A Title command fixes the labels of the worksheet in place on the screen as you scroll through other parts of the sheet. Using this command, you could scroll to a specific portion of a worksheet and view it, or even print it with the labels showing.

The editing commands Blank and Clear are useful but potentially dangerous. Blank erases the contents of a cell, and Clear erases the whole worksheet. Before erasing the worksheet, however, the program prompts you to confirm whether you want to take such drastic action.

Once you create a worksheet, you normally save it on disk. The Storage command enables you to save your worksheet on a disk, load a worksheet into the PC from a disk, and carry out several other routine file-handling functions. One useful feature of the Storage command is the Data Interchange Format (DIF) for files. Files stored in this special format can be used by other VisiCorp applications programs, such as *VisiTrend/Plot,* a business graphics program. Programs from other manufacturers can also usually read DIF files, primarily because the original *VisiCalc* program was so popular. Most spreadsheet programs have similar utilities for file interchange.

With the worksheet built, you can then print it on paper. The Print command enables you to use a variety of printers. Although *VisiCalc* contains printer control codes that determine various printing characteristics such as type size, the codes are not stored as part of the worksheet and must be entered before each printing. Newer versions of *VisiCalc* and other spreadsheet programs have corrected this deficiency.

Recent Spreadsheet Enhancements

SuperCalc (Sorcim), introduced about a year after *VisiCalc,* made some significant improvements to an already good program. Most of *SuperCalc*'s improved features involve formatting. With *SuperCalc,* you can format a range of cells without using the Replicate command. You can also either protect a cell or a range of cells so that its contents cannot accidentally be changed, or hide a cell or a range of cells so it will not appear in the spreadsheet, even though it is used in calculations.

SuperCalc is easier to use than *VisiCalc.* It provides error messages in plain English and a Help command that displays simple explanations. *SuperCalc* also provides a limited capability to store a series of commands in a worksheet with the Alternate Input command. You can put together a series of *SuperCalc* commands and enter them into the worksheet as a data file rather than reentering them. In this way, you can automate routine, recurring tasks in setting up and editing a worksheet.

Although *CalcStar* (MicroPro) isn't as versatile as *SuperCalc* and *VisiCalc,* it does have a few unique features. It offers four statistical functions not found on other basic spreadsheets, most notably linear regression. The program can be used as a calculator, and it also allows you to enter text messages in cells, although these messages only appear when the cell is active, and they are not printed.

As good as basic spreadsheets are, they have significant limitations. More sophisticated programs such as *SuperCalc3* (Sorcim), *1-2-3* (Lotus Development), and *MBA* (Context Management Systems) are faster in most instances, easier to use, and have more features than their predecessors. Some of these programs are stand-alone spreadsheets and some are integrated programs that include other major applications such as business graphics and data management.

Formatting has been improved in the newer programs, with more options and some new features. For example, you can name cells or ranges of cells and then use the names instead of cell numbers in functions and formulas. This welcome step can help keep track of the meaning of complicated formulas that reference many cells. Second-generation spreadsheets give control of column width for individual cells, and several of the programs have limited text-handling capabilities that enable the user to type a long phrase on screen without having to divide it into chunks and enter the information one cell at a time. *1-2-3* and *VisiCalc Advanced Version* (Software Arts) also use *macros,* or sequences of commands that can be invoked with a single keystroke. With macros, an experienced spreadsheet user can both create templates for someone who has minimal knowledge of spreadsheets and automate complicated spreadsheet procedures into simpler ones. Some spreadsheet programs accomplish the same result with a "forms mode" that enables the user to create worksheets with a process similar to filling in the blanks on a form.

One of the most obvious enhancements in spreadsheets is increased capacity, which is achieved in two ways. Spreadsheets such as *1-2-3* and *MBA* are large; *1-2-3* provides about 30 times as many cells as the original *VisiCalc.* But there are subtler ways to expand the number of cells a program can use. *Multiplan,* for instance, has the ability to link worksheets and pass information between them. This linking feature is extremely useful, because it enables you to create worksheets that take their information from other worksheets. Not by accident, this process mirrors the way businesses consolidate subordinate financial reports into all-inclusive corporate documents.

As spreadsheet programs have evolved, many new mathematical functions have been added, especially business-related ones. Now available are functions that calculate future value, financial management rate of return, payment, interest rate, and internal rate of return. Especially useful for businesspeople are calendar functions, which apply date and time factors to investment analysis and other operations. Statistical and trigonometric functions have also been expanded in the more advanced spreadsheets.

Multiplan has an enhanced Lookup feature that enables it to work on tables much more complex than individual blocks of columns or rows. And many new programs can sort data numerically and alphabetically.

A trend with all applications programs—not just with spreadsheets—is increasing their ease of use. Command menus, on-screen help messages, and prompts are the rule rather than the exception in the current lineup of spreadsheets. Help screens are most often context sensitive—they automatically display information that relates to the topic at hand. And documentation is generally improving. Many spreadsheets are also incorporating the use of the latest input and control devices, such as the mouse.

Spreadsheet Uses

In general, spreadsheets are useful for recurring tasks for which you can create a model and enter new data as needed. In fact, any financial application that is subject to changes in key figures followed by long recalculations is a prime candidate for spreadsheets. A spreadsheet's ability to recalculate endlessly makes it especially useful for tasks that require scenario building or "what if" analysis.

Budgeting, often an exercise in "what if" analysis, is also an excellent use of spreadsheets. Financial forecasting is appropriate as well; the more uncertain your assumptions, the more valuable a spreadsheet is in evaluating numerous financial alternatives.

Spreadsheets are also handy for creating bids and proposals quickly, when fast turnaround and the ability to adjust figures rapidly is important. You can perform almost any type of investment analysis with a spreadsheet, such as lease versus buy, break-even, and return on investment. Of course, planning and calculating your taxes are especially useful applications for spreadsheets.

Spreadsheets created the revolution in personal computers, and they undoubtedly will continue to be among the most popular and useful computer applications, especially for businesspeople. In the chapter that follows, you will become acquainted with two of the most popular spreadsheets for the IBM PC and XT: *Multiplan* and *SuperCalc3*.

CHAPTER THREE

An Introduction to Multiplan and SuperCalc3

Electronic spreadsheets have become popular because in many ways they resemble the calculation tools that businesspeople routinely use. The columns and rows of an electronic worksheet are similar to those of traditional ledger paper. Businesspeople can lay out information on screen the way they have on paper without having to learn complex data entry procedures.

The process of entering formulas in cells is similar to keying mathematical operations on a hand-held calculator. Once you get the hang of entering cell references rather than specific numbers in formulas, spreadsheet math is easy to understand and requires much less programming savvy than would be needed to program a similar math function in BASIC, for example.

You can create financial models on a spreadsheet, periodically insert weekly, monthly, or yearly figures, and watch the spreadsheet update the figures. And once you create an electronic worksheet, you are relieved of most of the burdensome "headwork" associated with juggling financial figures.

One of the best spreadsheet programs for the PC is *Multiplan* (Microsoft). It has many features that make it easy to use, especially compared to the original version of *VisiCalc*. Although *Multiplan* is only a spreadsheet and does not incorporate data base and graphics functions (except in a very limited way), the program offers flexibility and a full range of operations.

Another major contender in the spreadsheet competition is *SuperCalc3*. This program offers the basic spreadsheet features, as well as several advanced features that incorporate business graphics—a first step toward program integration. This chapter introduces *Multiplan* and *SuperCalc3*, both of which are valuable additions to any software library.

Multiplan

Multiplan is deservedly popular among microcomputer users. Not only does it improve the original spreadsheet concept, but it implements new features in a comprehensible way. *Multiplan*'s flexible and efficient features and ease of use have led to its widespread acceptance among PC and XT users.

Documentation The excellence of the overall package is reflected in the documentation and packaging. The program comes in a clear plastic box that converts into a stand for the user guide and a storage compartment for the disks and other parts of the documentation.

Multiplan's manual is comprehensive but not especially easy to use. Consisting of three major parts—a 188-page tutorial, a reference section, and several appendices—it is bound in a three-ring binder, is typeset, and has excellent illustrations and screen examples. The tutorial begins with a chapter on program fundamentals, explaining the use of the spreadsheet screen. It leads you through the process of building a worksheet, formatting columns and rows, entering formulas, and using editing procedures.

The manual introduces *Multiplan*'s advanced features, including naming ranges of cells to simplify spreadsheet math, splitting the screen into multiple windows, and printing reports, and it includes a section on advanced problem-solving techniques. The writing is clear, jargon is kept to a minimum, and the common mistakes a user might make are often anticipated and explained. The reference section includes chapters detailing the commands, the editing operations, the use of formulas, and file-handling procedures. An alphabetized listing of program commands and a listing of *Multiplan*'s math functions are also included. The listings provide instructions for using particular commands or functions.

The documentation includes a customer service plan; a quick reference guide to keyboard functions, commands, formulas, functions, and error codes; and a demonstration kit for *Multiplan* applications *Budget* and *Financial Statements,* which augment the *Multiplan* program and must be purchased separately. Included with the demo package is a disk that comes with two sample templates.

Features *Multiplan* is a reliable product that introduces some outstanding spreadsheet features. It departs in several ways from the original *VisiCalc* design, most often to make worksheet production easier or more flexible. Although *Multiplan,* like many other spreadsheets, can handle worksheets of 63 columns and 255 rows, the grid is labeled differently. *Multiplan* uses numbers for both columns and rows, rather than the more common convention of numbers for rows, and letters for columns. *Multiplan* also reverses the order of reference for columns and rows by referring to rows first. (Those who are accustomed to a letter-number combination in column-row order may be confused by this.) The first cell in *Multiplan* is R1C1 (row 1, column 1), while *VisiCalc*'s first cell is A1 (column A, row 1).

The *Multiplan* screen is easier to understand for first-time spreadsheet users than *VisiCalc*'s abbreviated style of displaying information. Whereas *VisiCalc's* command line is a row of single letters stretching across the screen, *Multiplan* provides a menu of commands written out as whole words. *Multiplan* provides information about the amount of memory available, easily understandable error messages, and prompts that instruct the user during editing procedures. Even with all this information, 7 columns and 20 rows are visible at one time on the standard single-window screen (see Figure 3.1).

Multiplan is menu-driven, and the command menu is displayed on two lines at the bottom of the screen. Just under the command menu is a message line that displays prompts and error messages. On the bottom line, or the status line, the location and the contents of the active cell are displayed, along with the amount of memory available and the name of the current worksheet.

#1	1	2	3	4	5	6	7
1		January	February	March	April	May	June
2							
3	Sales	$20000.00	$20000.00	$20000.00	$20000.00	$20000.00	$2000.00
4							
5	Cost						
6	Material	$4000.00	$4000.00	$4600.00	$4000.00	$4500.00	$4000.00
7	Labor	$7000.00	$7000.00	$7000.00	$7000.00	$7000.00	$7000.00
8	Overhead	$4000.00	$4000.00	$4000.00	$4000.00	$4000.00	$4000.00
9		--------------	--------------	--------------	--------------	--------------	--------------
10	Total Costs	$15000.00	$15000.00	$15600.00	$15000.00	$15500.00	$1500.00
11							
12							
13							
14							
15	NET	$5000.00	$5000.00	$4400.00	$5000.00	$4500.00	$5000.00
16							
17							
18							
19							
20							

COMMAND: Alpha Blank Copy Delete Edit Format Goto Help Insert Lock Move
Name Options Print Quit Sort Transfer Value Window Xternal
Select option or type command letter
R3C2 20000 99% Free Multiplan: spencer

Figure 3.1 Multiplan's *standard worksheet display. The cursor is indicated by the box around $20000.00 under January; the text at the bottom of the screen shows commands and cursor location.*

Multiplan makes good use of the PC function keys, including the cursor movement keys. You can scroll through the worksheet vertically or horizontally, using the cursor control keys or the <Home>, <End>, <PgUp>, or <PgDn> keys. The program also offers a quick way to move to specific spots on the worksheet with a Goto command. You can use this command to move the cursor to a specific cell, a range of cells, a window, or a specified area of the worksheet.

There are two common ways to reference cells in *Multiplan* formulas: with absolute cell references and with relative cell references. Absolute references include the actual coordinates of cells in the formula, such as R6C2 = R4C2 + R5C2.

Formulas that have absolute cell references always use information from the specific cells identified in the formula. If you change the layout of the worksheet by adding rows or columns, the formulas will not adjust to the insertion of other cells. If you were to add a row between the current rows 4 and 5 in the example above, the formula would still add R4C2 to R5C2, even though R5C2 is really now R6C2. If you copied the formula to other cells, it would still total only the originally specified cells, R4C2 and R5C2. This type of formula cannot be copied and used repetitively to build a worksheet, because the result is always the sum of the same two cells.

Relative cell referencing enables you to rearrange the worksheet easily and have formulas automatically adjust to new layouts. A relative reference defines cells used in formulas in terms of their distance and direction from the cell containing the formula, or the active cell.

If you wanted to define cell R6C2 as the sum of cells R4C2 and R5C2, the value of cell R6C2 would be the sum of the values in the cell two rows above R6C2 and the cell one row above R6C2. The relative reference would be R[–2]C + R[–1]C. Once you have constructed this formula based on the relative position of the active cell, it doesn't matter what you do to rearrange the worksheet; the formula will always adjust and use the correct cells. If you created a formula that had relative cell referencing that adds up a column of figures, for example, you could copy the formula to other columns, and it would total each of the other columns. Using relative cell referencing relieves you of having to create the same formula repeatedly in different cells; you can just copy the appropriate formula into them.

Multiplan also enables you to construct formulas on the screen using the cursor keys to point to specific cells required in a formula. You don't have to type a cell reference; you can simply point to it from the cursor, and *Multiplan* will insert the cell reference in the formula. With the previous example, you would begin by positioning the cursor on cell R6C2 and entering an equal sign. This action would alert the program that you are building a formula, not a label. You would then move the cursor to cell R4C2. You would see the first element of your formula, R[–2]C, appear at the status line. Wanting to add another cell reference, you would type a plus sign. The cursor would jump back automatically to the active cell, R6C2. You would then move the cursor to cell R5C2 and press <Enter>, to complete the formula that adds R4C2 to R5C2. The cursor would move back to the active cell, and your formula would be displayed in its entirety on the status line, saving you from having to type a single cell reference.

You can name groups of cells, such as a row of related figures, and use the cell name when creating formulas. Naming cells is an efficient way to reference areas of a worksheet without having to enter lengthy sets of cell coordinates in a formula. For instance, you might name an entire row of a worksheet "Costs" and another row of figures "Sales"; then you could create a formula to calculate profit by simply entering the formula "Sales–Costs." This method of creating spreadsheet formulas is ultimately more useful for businesspeople than the method of using abstract cell references.

Multiplan's normal cell width is 10 characters. You can set a specific width for one column, for a range of columns, or for all columns on the worksheet. Within a cell, you can also control how the contents are displayed. Labels and figures can be shown centered, flush left or right, or with text displayed flush left and numbers flush right. Numbers can be displayed as percentages, dollar amounts, integers, or in other notation such as scientific, fixed point, or even a simple graph.

Multiplan really shines when it comes to windows. The program can support up to eight windows at once, split either horizontally or vertically (see Figure 3.2). You can scroll inside each window either horizontally or vertically and "lock" titles in place on rows or columns using the Window command.

You can also add borders around any window—in color if you like. You can use color as an identifier by color coding windows displaying data that has special meaning. For instance, you might assign different colors to data from different divisions of a company or different regions, or use colored windows to delineate areas of the worksheet that you don't want changed. *Multiplan* lets you choose from 15 colors when you are using the Window Paint command. (Of course, your computer must have a color graphics board and a color monitor to utilize these features.)

```
#1    1        #2      2          3           4           5           6
 1                  January   February      March       April        May
 2
 3  Sales          $20000.00  $20000.00  $20000.00  $20000.00  $20000.00
 4
 5  Cost
 6          Material $4000.00   $4000.00   $4600.00   $4000.00   $4500.00
 7             Labor $7000.00   $7000.00   $7000.00   $7000.00   $7000.00
 8          Overhead $4000.00   $4000.00   $4000.00   $4000.00   $4000.00
 9                  -----------------------------------------------------
10       Total Costs $15000.00 $15000.00  $15600.00  $15000.00  $15500.00
11
12            #3       7          8           9          10          11
13            11
14            12
15  NET       13
16            14
17            15   $5000.00   $5000.00   $5000.00   $5000.00   $5000.00
18            16
19            17
20
COMMAND: Alpha Blank Copy Delete Edit Format Goto Help Insert Lock Move
         Name Options Print Quit Sort Transfer Value Window Xternal
Select option or type command letter
R3C2        20000                   99% Free            Multiplan: spencer
```

Figure 3.2 *A Multiplan screen with three windows: #1 indicates the column containing labels, #2 shows adjacent columns, and #3 shows columns 7 through 11 and rows 11 through 17.*

Multiplan has a wide range of enhanced formatting features, including the ability to format individual cells, ranges of cells, columns, whole worksheets, and printed reports. Formatting printed worksheets is easy with *Multiplan.* Using the Print Margins command, you can set the values for the left and top margins, the length and the width of the printed area, and the page length.

Multiplan has 40 mathematical functions, 12 of which were not in the original version of *VisiCalc.* Several new functions deal with formatting. For instance, a Fixed function converts numbers to text format so you can use them in titles and labels. A Dollar function converts dollar amounts to text showing a dollar amount. If the amount is negative, *Multiplan* puts parentheses around the text amount.

Several data management features of the program give it the capabilities of a simple list manager. Lookup tables and indexed tables enable *Multiplan* to locate and use specific data from predefined lists of data. You can also sort tables and columns in ascending or descending order, either alphabetically or numerically.

Although *Multiplan* can address only 64K of memory at once, limiting the potential size of a worksheet, the program has a way of skirting this apparent deficiency. You can link worksheets using the External command so that they share information as if they were one large spreadsheet. Data can then be transferred between sheets and automatically updated. This linking feature provides tremendous flexibility in designing and working with large models and is good for dealing with worksheets that depend upon other worksheets for supporting data.

Multiplan's menu structure is easy to use. You choose a command from the command menu by either typing the first letter of the command, such as P for Print, or moving the edit cursor to the desired command with the space bar and pressing <Enter>. Submenus providing other options then appear. Once in the submenu, you move from field to field with the <Tab> key and fill in command fields or respond to prompts. You can cancel any command by pressing <Esc> and automatically return to the initial command menu.

Multiplan provides a good help facility. You can choose the Help command from the command menu, or press the question mark key from any of the submenus. A help message is displayed that explains the particular command you are using. Error messages provide clear descriptions and adequate information.

Support Microsoft supports the program with a 90-day limited warranty. If the program proves defective within that period, the company will replace it. Although the company offers a customer support hot line to help with technical questions, it is not a toll-free number. *Multiplan* owners are notified of new versions and are offered a chance to purchase them at a reduced price.

There are no special hardware requirements for *Multiplan.* In fact, the program will run on a PC that has the minimum configuration: 128K of RAM and one disk drive.

Multiplan is an excellent product. You might fault the program for not having other applications integrated into it, but it has many desirable spreadsheet features and is a pleasure to use.

SuperCalc3

SuperCalc3 is the third incarnation of *SuperCalc,* the first spreadsheet to make significant improvements over the original *VisiCalc* design. *SuperCalc3* has most of the advanced features of a modern spreadsheet and an integrated business graphics function that can be accessed directly from the spreadsheet.

Documentation The documentation for *SuperCalc3* includes a manual; a tutorial called "10 Minutes to SuperCalc3"; reference cards for the program's menus, commands, formulas, and functions as well as the graphics features and functions; and another manual for a data conversion program called SuperData Interchange.

The manual is spiral bound, so it lies flat on the desk as you work with the program. Although the text is both well written and well organized, the index could be more comprehensive. The tutorial provides a quick tour of the program's features, including building, editing, and printing a worksheet, and creating a graph from the worksheet data. Although "10 Minutes to SuperCalc3" is an effective confidence builder, the manual itself is good enough that you might just start with it. The quick-reference cards are well executed and helpful.

Features Anyone who has used *VisiCalc* will recognize the *SuperCalc3* screen right away. It has the familiar spreadsheet layout of 8 columns and 20 rows, with rows numbered and columns indicated by letters. The total worksheet area is 63 columns by 254 rows. There are three lines of information

```
    |      A      ||     B      ||     C      ||     D      ||     E      ||     F      |
  1 | Income Statement
  2 |
  3 |                    Q1            Q2            Q3            Q4            Year
  4 |              ____________________________________________________________________
  5 | Sales            25000         20000         35000         25000        105000
  6 | Costs           [15000]        12000         21000         15000         63000
  7 |
  8 | NET              10000          8000         14000         10000         42000
  9
 10
 11
 12
 13
 14
 15
 16
 17
 18
 19
 20
>B6            Form = 60%B5
Width: 12     Memory:125 Last Col/Row:G8          ? for HELP
   1>__
F1=Help; F2=Erase Line/Return to Spreadsheet; F9=Plot; F10=View
```

Figure 3.3 *The standard screen for* SuperCalc3. *The program is in data entry mode; the edit cursor is shown in the line next to the bottom beside the '>' prompt.*

near the bottom of the screen: status, prompt, and entry (see Figure 3.3).

The first item on the status line indicates the direction of the cursor. In *SuperCalc3,* the cursor moves automatically one cell in the direction indicated on the status line when you press <Enter>, but you can turn off this feature if you like. The next item shows the location of the active cell. Next to the active cell indicator, format options set for the active cell are displayed. This information includes a designation of whether the contents of the active cell are text or a formula, and whether the active cell is protected and cannot be changed inadvertently. The contents of the cell are also displayed. But because so much information is displayed in this one line, it can be confusing and difficult to decipher.

SuperCalc3 has three different modes, and the prompt line indicates the current mode. If it is in "data entry" mode, the prompt line displays the column width of the active cell, the amount of available program memory, and the location of the last cell that contains data. If the program is in "command" mode, the prompt line displays the current prompt, and you can execute commands to do such things as switch windows, go to a specific cell location, or recalculate the values in the worksheet. The third mode, or "spreadsheet" mode, enables you to move the cursor around the spreadsheet to view cell contents and values. The last element on the prompt line is the question mark, which you use to get help.

The entry line displays the data entered in the active cell. The first character that you type indicates the kind of entry: formula, text, or command. When you are in data entry mode, the active cursor, called the edit cursor, appears in this line.

At the bottom of the screen is a list of function keys, which are used to summon help, erase a data or command entry that has not yet been entered, plot a graph, or view a graph. *SuperCalc3* is command-driven; you type a slash and a letter to execute each command. When executing a command, the program displays prompts on the screen to guide you through its procedures.

Cursor movement in *SuperCalc3* is not particularly powerful. With the program in spreadsheet mode, you can move the cursor by using the cursor keys or by typing <Ctrl>-key combinations, such as <Ctrl>-E, <Ctrl>-X, <Ctrl>-S, or <Ctrl>-D to move the cursor up, down, left, or right, respectively. The <Home> key moves the cursor to cell A1, but the <End> key isn't used. You can scroll with the cursor keys or with <Ctrl>-key combinations. (The program does not use <PgUp> and <PgDn> keys.) The program has a Goto command for moving the cursor directly to any cell on the worksheet.

Moving the cursor in two ways—using the function keys or the <Ctrl>-key combinations—is a holdover from *SuperCalc*'s development as a CP/M-based program, in which standard cursor keys were not always used. Learning two ways to move the cursor offers flexibility, and you can generally choose the way you like best.

SuperCalc3 has all the basic spreadsheet features as well as some interesting advanced features. The program provides the standard logical functions. In addition to the Boolean operators "if," "or," "and," and "not" are a wide array of financial functions, including net present value, internal rate of return, payment, future value, and present value. These functions make *SuperCalc3* a particularly good choice for business use. The program also has calendar functions for date arithmetic and for automatically entering dates into the worksheet. Once dates are entered, you can do mathematical operations based on them, and you can use dates in lookup tables.

A special feature of *SuperCalc3* enables you to display text as results of logical functions and lookup tables. A certain selection mode made by a Lookup function might display a message rather than a number. Text can also be used with the "if" function. For example, you might type B3 = IF(A1>1000,"GREAT","TOO BAD"). In this formula, if the value of cell A1 is greater than 1000, the word "Great" will be displayed in cell B3. If A1 has a value less than or equal to 1000, the words "Too Bad" will be displayed.

SuperCalc3 can also sort information. The program uses the Arrange command to sort the worksheet, based on the values of one or two rows or columns. You can sort either alphabetically or numerically, in ascending or descending order. You have to be careful with *SuperCalc3*'s sort order, however. If you sort in ascending order, the data will be arranged in the following sequence: spaces first, then other nonnumeric, non-alphabetic characters (such as punctuation marks), then alphabetic characters (with lowercase letters before their uppercase counterparts), and finally numbers. For example, an entry that started with a space followed by a *Z* would appear before an entry starting with an *A* after sorting by *SuperCalc3*. (This problem is more or less typical of computer sorting, however.)

Although not as flexible at formatting as *Multiplan, SuperCalc3* has some useful formatting features. Text entries too long to fit into one cell can run over into blank columns. You can also vary the width of individual columns. Although *SuperCalc3* offers a window feature, the program supports only two windows. You can protect a cell from being altered, and in a related feature you can "hide" the contents of a cell so they won't be displayed or printed and protect the confidentiality of some figures. The cell contents will still be a functioning part of the worksheet; if the contents are a formula, you can see the formula on the status line, but the value won't be displayed.

SuperCalc3 enables you to program or automate some spreadsheet functions using the Execute command. With this feature, you can create a new command composed of a series of *SuperCalc3* commands, save it on disk, and later execute the series as if it were only one command. This is an extremely useful feature that enables you to create editing tools to help speed up the worksheet process. The only editing procedures you can't control with an Execute file are entering data and editing entries, but the program offers a simple way to interrupt and resume the Execute operation automatically so you can enter data from the keyboard. This feature enables you to create "turnkey" spreadsheet operations that require operator input for only data entry.

One of *SuperCalc3*'s most valuable features is its ability to combine worksheets and perform arithmetic operations during the combination. The Consolidate option of the Load command adds the contents of identical cells from two worksheets to form one consolidated sheet. This is very useful for companies that have several divisions that each prepare different but identically formatted spreadsheets. You can also graph the consolidated worksheets if you want to.

SuperCalc3 files are stored in a special binary format that can't be read by other programs, but the program provides SuperData Interchange, a utility for converting *SuperCalc3* files into formats that use ASCII characters. SuperData Interchange can convert *SuperCalc3* files into two types of files: comma-separated value files and SuperData Interchange format files. Comma-separated value files are used by many data base management programs, and the SuperData Interchange format is similar to the DIF file available with *VisiCalc*. SuperData Interchange can also convert comma-separated value, DIF, and *VisiCalc* files directly into *SuperCalc3* format. The conversion is easy to perform, and the program uses menus and prompts to guide you through the process.

SuperCalc3's built-in business graphics couldn't be easier to use. You can create seven types of graphs: pie, bar, line, stacked bar, area, XY, and high-low-close. You can also create color graphs that have headings and labels. The program can display basic graphics on the IBM Monochrome Display or another monitor without requiring a color graphics board.

Once you have determined which elements of a worksheet you want to graph, you access graphics with the View command. The program prompts you to enter data for several graphing variables, such as graph type, data, labels, and headings. You use the information in cells of the worksheet for labels and headings, although you can define your own by adding information to the worksheet if the labels you want aren't already there. Labels print horizontally or vertically, and you can choose from among eight type fonts. If you get confused at any time during the graphing process, on-screen help is available. The help messages provide a summary of the current graph description and a general description of graphics features.

Once you have defined the graph, the graphics description is saved on disk along with the worksheet. Up to nine graphs can be stored with each worksheet. You can print or plot a graph, delete a graph description, and copy graph descriptions from one graph to another to avoid rekeying information.

SuperCalc3's business graphics compare well with many stand-alone business graphics packages. And the convenience of producing them so easily makes the package a real standout. This program provides one of the clearest examples of the convenience provided by integrating several functions into a single package.

Support Like most software publishers, Sorcim offers a 90-day warranty with *SuperCalc3*. Although the company provides telephone assistance during weekday business hours, the service does not offer a toll-free number. Sorcim also publishes a quarterly magazine that features articles and tips about the firm's software.

CHAPTER FOUR

Word Processing

A good word processing program would be worth its price if all it did were to help you write more easily. But writing (entering) and editing are only two of the five major text processing tasks that word processors handle. Word processing also automates file handling, text formatting, and printing.

Creating a draft document on a personal computer with a word processing program is similar to working with a typewriter in that you type text on a keyboard. But in some ways the PC keyboard is even better than a typewriter, because it has keys that can be dedicated to specific functions. Using these keys or specific commands, you can move quickly to any point in the text and delete letters, words, sentences, paragraphs, or even the complete document. You can insert characters, words, or large blocks of text anywhere within a document and move sections of text to new positions. These "cut-and-paste" operations can be executed with a few keystrokes, and a good feature of some word processing programs is automatic reformatting of the text to accommodate the changes.

A Summary of Word Processing Features

The basic editing tasks are inserting, deleting, overtyping, copying, moving, searching and replacing, and windowing. Some programs can even restore deleted text.

File-handling features provide the capability of storing and retrieving work on disk electronically. The program can transfer text to a disk, where it is recorded under a file name that you assign. After storing your work on disk, you can use the program to create other documents, print your work, or run other programs. Later, you can read the document again for further editing or printing. Word processing programs also enable you to delete documents, give them new names, and copy files onto other disks for safekeeping.

Word processing programs provide various features for formatting text the way you want it to appear on paper. As with a typewriter, you can set margins, pitch, and line spacing, but many programs have more powerful formatting features that enable you to do such things as create justified text (flush left and right along the margins), and print text with proportional spacing (characters are allocated different spacing according to their individual widths).

Word processing programs differ in the ways in which they display text. Some feature true on-screen formatting—"what you see is what you get." You arrange the text on screen as you want it to appear on paper; when you print the text, it follows the on-screen format. Other programs display text unformatted; you have to insert formatting codes in the text for such things as margin changes, line spacing, and indentations. On screen the text does not appear as it will print on paper. This type of program requires a separate formatting step—after the text is created, but before printing. After the formatting step, you can usually view a copy of the formatted text on the screen before printing it.

The most common printing you will do is on paper, or "hard copy." Although most word processors offer many printing features, such as underlining, italics, and subscripts and superscripts, you must be sure that the printer you use is compatible with the specific program you have. Although most word processing programs can use almost any popular printer, if you have a specialized printer, the program may not be able to take advantage of its features or even communicate with it.

Menus vs. Commands

Although most word processing programs for the IBM PC have the same basic features, each program is organized differently. Word processors generally fall into one of two categories: menu-driven and command-driven (also referred to as menu-based and command-based).

WordStar (MicroPro) is primarily a command-driven program. In order to put the program through its paces, you have to learn many commands that are difficult to remember. *Microsoft Word,* on the other hand, is a menu-driven program. *Word*'s commands are organized into menus, or lists of commands that perform word processing functions. Menu-driven programs typically have a main menu that accesses the major functions, such as editing, formatting, and printing. By choosing one of the main menu functions, you are presented with a submenu of related functions. If you select the print option from the main menu, for example, you might be presented with a submenu that has options for printing to a disk, on paper, or to the screen.

Some menu-driven programs offer more than one way to select menu items. For example, with *Word* you can either type the first letter of the menu item or move the cursor to the desired option and press <Enter>. Some word processing programs, including *Word,* incorporate a mouse, an electronic pointing device that enables you to make rapid menu selections. To select a menu item with a mouse, you move the mouse along the desktop until its corresponding on-screen pointer is on the menu item, then push a button on the mouse to implement a desired action.

Menu-based programs are easier to use than command-based programs, because they provide information when you need it. Once you learn a menu-based program thoroughly, however, you may find that the menus slow you down as you try to navigate quickly through many selections. It can be irritating to plow through layer upon layer of prompts, messages, and menus. Also, menus take up valuable display space, usually at least two full lines. The ideal program would have extensive menus and prompts that could be suppressed at will. It would be easy to learn, but the experienced user could streamline the program for speed and power. *WordStar* provides on-screen help information that can be turned on or off.

Cursor Movement

The basic work area for a word processor is the edit screen. You type in text, edit and format it, save it on disk, and print it. Depending on how much other information—such as menus, prompts, and messages—is on the screen, an edit screen usually holds about 20 to 22 lines of text. You may also see various borders and rulers that help with formatting. For each of these options, the cursor is your guide.

Ease of cursor movement is important in a word processing program, because editing requires that you use the cursor frequently. Different word processing programs move the cursor in different ways. Most programs use the cursor keys on the numeric keypad, which move the cursor up, down, left, and right. These keys also repeat; if you hold them down, the cursor will move continuously in the desired direction.

With most word processors, the <Backspace> key moves the cursor one space to the left and deletes the character in that place. In all programs, the space bar moves the cursor one space to the right, but it inserts blank spaces as it goes or erases letters as the cursor passes over them. For this reason, you rarely use the space bar to move the cursor. Cursor keys, a command, or a mouse move the cursor where you want it to go.

The best word processors have commands that move the cursor a word, a line, or a paragraph at a time. The PC has two keys dedicated solely to cursor movement. Depending on the way a program uses it, the <Home> key moves the cursor to the beginning of the current line, the top of the screen, or the beginning of the document. In similar fashion, the <End> key moves the cursor to the end of the current line, the end of the screen, or the end of the document. Some programs have methods of moving the cursor to a specified page in a document or to another designated point that can be set. Because cursor movement is a critical word processing feature, choose a program that offers maximum flexibility in this area.

Scrolling Closely related to cursor control is a feature called scrolling. As you enter text on the edit screen, you can quickly fill up the available space. As you continue typing, the program automatically provides additional space at the bottom of the screen by moving several lines of text off the top.

You can scroll through a document using the PC's dedicated scrolling keys. The <PgUp> (page up) key enables you to bring the previous screen into view, and the <PgDn> (page down) key calls up the following screen. Some programs allow continuous scrolling at different speeds and horizontal as well as vertical scrolling to show text beyond the width of the screen.

Word wrap One of the first features you notice when you begin to use a word processor is *word wrap.* You can type text continuously without having to press <Enter> at the end of each line. Words that would otherwise extend past the right margin are automatically moved to the next line. Carriage returns (pressing <Enter>) are necessary only between paragraphs.

Inserting and Deleting Text

Every program has a dominant, or *default,* mode as well as other modes that you can access. *Insert* is a common default mode. When the program is in this mode, you can insert text in a document, and the program automatically moves text to the right to accommodate the new entry (see Figure 4.1). Many programs often have other editing modes, such as delete, or overtype, which substitutes whatever new text you enter for the text that occupied that exact location on the screen (see Figure 4.2). The program usually helps you keep track of

Figure 4.1 *An example of insert mode in* WordStar. *The word "automatically" has been added to the bottom sentence, and the text following it has been moved to the right.*

```
          B:File PAGE 1 LINE 2 COL 35        INSERT ON
L----!----!----!----!----!----!---R

When the program is in insert mode,
the program moves text to the
right.

When the program is in insert mode,
the program automaticallymoves text to the right.
```

```
B:File PAGE 1 LINE 2 COL 35
L----!----!----!----!----!----!---R

When the program is in delete, or
overtype, mode, the program
types over old text with whatever
new text you type.

When the program is in delete, or
overtype, mode, the program
replaceyer old text with whatever
new text you type.
```

Figure 4.2 *An example of overtype mode in* Word-Star. *In the bottom sentence, the word "replace" has replaced the first seven characters of the third line.*

which mode you are in with an on-screen message. Generally, the fewer mode changes you have to make during editing, the better.

With many programs, switching out of insert mode puts the program in overtype mode. In that mode, you can replace any character at the cursor location by typing a new character. In most programs, overtype mode does not include automatic reformatting. If you use the <Backspace> key to delete a character while in overtype mode, for example, the program leaves a blank space to the left of the cursor and does not reformat the text to the right.

Most word processors have several keys that control text deletion. In many programs the <Backspace> key deletes characters to the left of the cursor, the <Delete> key erases any character the cursor is on, and function keys often control the deletion of lines and parts of lines. Most programs also provide commands for deleting blocks of text or (in extreme cases) all the text. Although many programs can't restore text that has been deleted, a few can. With such a program, whatever you have just deleted is stored in a memory buffer and remains there until you delete material at another cursor location. At that point, the buffer is cleared, and the new deletion is stored. With a program such as *Word,* you can restore whatever text is in the buffer.

Locating and Moving Text

Moving and copying blocks of text are two of the most useful features that word processing has to offer. Moving and copying are sometimes called "cut-and-paste" functions, because they replace tasks that editors and writers previously performed with scissors and paste or tape. To move a block of text, you designate the beginning and the end of the text to be moved, move the cursor to where the block is to appear, and execute a move command. The block disappears and reappears in a new position in the document. Most programs automatically reformat your text after a block move.

The amount of text you can move or copy is generally limited by the capacity of the particular program and the internal memory of the PC. Some programs can move and copy columns as well as regular text.

Two other useful editing tools are search and replace. When using the search feature, you can isolate a character or string of characters and tell the program to find every occurrence in the document. You can specify individual words or phrases and have the computer search for them. This feature is especially useful for getting to specific points quickly in a lengthy document.

The search and replace feature enables you to find repeated occurrences of words or characters and replace them. If a misspelled word appears many times throughout a document, for example, you can use search and replace to change every occurrence of the misspelling without having to do each correction individually or manually.

There are clever ways to use search and replace. For instance, you can flag a section of text that you want to expand upon later by marking it with a symbol. Later, you can write the added material and have the program substitute it for the designated symbol. Or substitute a symbol for a frequently used name or number that is difficult or time-consuming to type, then type it once and have the program replace the symbol everywhere it occurs in one easy step.

Windowing, or splitting the screen into two or more subdivisions, is a feature that some new word processors have, especially those that use the mouse for cursor control. Windowing refers to the ability of a program to split the editing screen and display different sections of text simultaneously. You can create several windows and within each window view separate documents or different parts of the same document. In some programs you can even scroll independently in each window. Although windows are handy for making simultaneous revisions, one of the best uses for windows is block moves between separate documents.

File Management

With most word processing programs, you can easily store text on disk, list all the files you have stored on a disk, and see how much space you still have available on a disk. Good programs work interactively with PC-DOS to facilitate the saving process (you don't have to leave the program to save a document).

A word processing program should help you circumvent the dreaded "Disk Full" condition (when you have created a document but cannot save it because the disk is full). A good program offers ample warning that you are running out of space, so you can take steps to avoid the problem or insert a new disk if the current one is full.

Another way to avoid the problem is to work with small documents. Unfortunately, working with many short documents can be troublesome, especially when you have to print them out as one long document. Many word processors have procedures for appending documents—you can make a consolidated final version from many smaller parts. The append feature is also handy for inserting "boilerplate," or frequently used, paragraphs in material such as contracts or proposals. You can also use it to create personalized mailings.

Some programs, such as *WordStar,* feature automatic disk buffering. The program loads only a portion of a document at a time into memory for editing, and when you are finished with that piece, it goes to disk and a new segment is loaded into memory for editing. Although this feature is handy if you work with long documents, it can slow the program down, because the disk has to be accessed frequently.

Formatting Text for Printing

Formatting is the process of setting up the layout of a document to determine line spacing, margins, justification, and so on. Word processing programs offer many formatting features. Some of these features, notably proportional spacing and full justification, can give text a typeset look.

When it comes to formatting, there are two types of word processors. As noted previously, true on-screen formatting displays text on the screen exactly as it will be printed. Other programs display the format commands you have entered, but the text does not appear as it will look in final form. Although you can adjust to either system, on-screen formatting is clearly easier to use.

Although most programs have preset format values, or default settings, you can usually change them to suit your needs. The better programs enable you to store your preferential settings and use them again. If you routinely use two sizes of stationery, for example, you can create two formats, each of which specifies the appropriate margins and number of lines to be printed on one size of paper.

The default setting for line spacing is most often single-spacing, but you should be able to change easily to double-spacing or any other units of spacing. Although ragged right is a common default setting, the more sophisticated programs can also justify the right margin.

Word processors perform full justification by using incremental spacing—inserting small spaces between characters. (Not all printers can support incremental spacing, however.) Occasionally justified text has unacceptably wide spaces between words. Although you can usually remedy this problem using hyphenation, be careful, because every word processing program handles hyphenation differently.

Most word processing programs allow you to print at 10, 12, or 15 characters per inch. The number of printed lines per page can be set according to paper size. Although the right margin is usually set at column 65 for normal 8½-by-11-inch paper, for wider paper you can set wider right margins.

Although some programs automatically set page breaks (depending on the number of lines you've set to be printed per page), you can usually override this feature and set page breaks manually with a specific command (called "forcing a page"). Often the page number does not show on the screen but appears on the printed document.

Whenever you change a format default setting, the program should indicate the change with some type of on-screen message. You can usually make as many format changes as you like within a document.

Many programs have features for automatically centering a line of text, aligning columns of numbers on a decimal point, or right justifying a column of words or numbers. These functions, if present, are often assigned to the function keys.

Some word processing programs provide "widow and orphan control." A "widow" or "orphan" is a line of text on a page separated from the rest of its paragraph on another page. You can avoid having lonely lines by inserting page breaks before or after them, respectively. Some programs automatically prevent stranded lines.

Most programs enable you to add headers and footers to documents. Headers and footers are labels or titles that you type once and are then repeated at the top and the bottom of every printed page.

Printing Text

Although manufacturers are quick to point out all the special printing features of their printers, many of those features are controlled by the word processing program. If your program doesn't support a particular feature, you can't use it, even if your printer is capable of performing it.

The most common printing features supported by word processors include underlining, boldface, italics, superscripts and subscripts, and special characters. Some of these features are controlled by function keys while others require commands. Underlining is usually accessed by a function key, for example. Many printers offer other printing enhancements, but to use them you have to send the printer special instruction called *setup strings,* sequences of characters that the printer will recognize as an instruction to implement a special printing attribute.

Although most word processors cannot display printing features such as underlining on screen, some programs mark the affected text, perhaps in inverse video, and display an on-screen message about the feature when the cursor is on the text marked. Programs that use embedded commands instead of on-screen formatting display the printing commands wherever you have inserted them. Some of the newest programs, such as *Word,* display the text exactly as it will print on paper, including italics and boldface. (This feature usually requires that the computer have a graphics board and a graphics display monitor.)

When you are finished editing a document, you can either print it, or store it as a text file and print it later. Some programs enable you to edit one file while printing another. You will appreciate this feature if you have a lot of work to do. Some programs also support *batch printing*—you can designate several different documents to be printed in sequence, in multiple copies, if necessary.

Word processors support a variety of printers: dot matrix, letter quality, normal and wide carriage, thermal, ink jet, and laser. If you need to use a specific printer that is not supported by your particular program, most programs will support it through a category called "any other printer." With this category you may be able to do basic printing, but you may not be able to take advantage of special printing attributes.

Auxiliary Programs

Word processing is such an important application that many programs have been developed to work with and enhance word processors. Three such applications are spelling checkers, style checkers, and mailing list programs.

A spelling checker compares your text with a "dictionary" of correctly spelled words and lists words that it interprets as possible misspellings. You can inspect each word and confirm whether the word is actually misspelled. If it is, the spelling checker will flag the word with a special symbol, and you can use the search feature of your word processor to find each misspelling and correct it. Some spelling checkers suggest alternate spellings and make corrections automatically. If you are a good speller, these programs may not be worth the time or the effort required, but most writers find them useful.

Although spelling checkers can't indicate poor writing style, a new type of program, called a style checker, can. These programs search the text and point out awkward constructions, overused words and phrases, and improper grammar. They may not be able to turn dull prose into dazzling writing, but they can be helpful for writers who are unsure of their grammar or style, or for those who have time constraints.

Mailing list programs work with word processing programs to produce mass mailings. Using the two programs interactively, you can personalize mailings by sending each person on a mailing list a letter that looks as if it came out of a typewriter. Mailing list programs can also be used as simple data base managers.

Word Processing Applications

Word processors are best for jobs that are fairly long and complex, or those that include other computer applications, such as spreadsheets or data base management. If you just want to produce a short letter or a memo, starting up a word processing program may not be worth the effort. But if you have a big job—and especially a repetitive one—there is nothing better.

Word processors are ideal for writing that must be perfect, or at least near perfect, and work that has to be produced under severe deadline pressure. Some examples are reports, books, newspaper and magazine articles, contracts, forms, legal briefs, speeches, and financial information, such as prospectuses and bond indentures.

Word processing is an application that alone justifies buying a PC. If you pick the right program, word processing can be easy to learn, and you will quickly find yourself doing productive work. The next chapter examines two programs that take very different approaches to this popular application.

CHAPTER FIVE

An Introduction to Microsoft Word and WordStar

For several years *WordStar* has been the most widely used word processing program for microcomputers. Not until recently have other word processing programs appeared on the market that rival *WordStar*'s reliability and performance. But one of the newest word processors for the PC and the XT promises to compete with *WordStar. Microsoft Word* (hereafter called *Word,*) is a powerful and innovative program, one of the first word processors to integrate mouse control with menu selection. And *Word* is specially designed to take advantage of the PC's features.

Microsoft Word

Word has many unique features. The program's cursor is different from that of most other word processing programs. *Word* uses a "selection," a cursor that can be directed through text and that can also simultaneously expand to mark words, sentences, lines, paragraphs, or even an entire document for editing operations such as copying or deleting.

By moving the mouse, you can swiftly move an arrow (or a rectangle, if you have a monochrome monitor) on the screen to different positions in the text. You can also scroll through the text and make menu selections with the mouse, minimizing the time required for many editing tasks. Although you can operate the program without the mouse, to get the full power of *Word,* you should use it. (You can purchase *Word* without the mouse, however.)

Because *Word* has so many features, it is not easy to master. Even for someone who has used several word processing programs, *Word*'s many procedures may take some time to learn.

Documentation Don't expect to get much help from the documentation. Although it is 399 pages long, the manual often answers questions insufficiently. Its organization is muddled, with most of the useful information at the back of the book. The most serious flaw is the lack of step-by-step instructions for *Word*'s procedures. The basic features of a program this complex should be explained clearly. But the manual provides just enough instruction to get you started with a function and then either leaves you hanging or refers to another section for further instructions. Despite an extensive index, finding answers to specific questions is difficult.

Although the manual includes a 65-page tutorial, you may finish it feeling as if you have not learned the basics. And parts of the tutorial are misleading. The section that explains scrolling using the mouse says that the on-screen pointer turns into a double-sided arrow when it is placed in the "scroll bar." This is true only if you are using a color/graphics board and the appropriate monitor. If you are using the IBM Monochrome Display, the pointer does not change shape. Someone using the Monochrome Display may be left wondering why the program doesn't work. In fact, the manual continually refers to the pointer as it would appear when the graphics board is being used, and ignores other configurations.

Overall, the documentation provides lots of instructions that are not very helpful. The manual for the mouse, however, is a marked improvement. It leads readers carefully through the steps of installing and using the mouse effectively.

Using the mouse The mouse is one of *Word*'s best features. You can buy it either packaged with the program or separately. To use the original Microsoft mouse, you have to install an interface board in the PC or the XT, but the installation instructions are excellent, and the entire procedure takes about five minutes. Microsoft is currently developing a mouse system that does not require a special interface board but connects to any serial port. At least one other mouse, the PC Mouse from Mouse Systems Corporation, also connects to a serial port and is compatible with *Word*.

You also have to run a mouse driver program, supplied on its own program disk, that you load before *Word*. Included on the disk are two practice programs that teach you how the mouse works. One program, "Piano," lets you play musical notes by "selecting" keys on a piano keyboard with the mouse—an amusing and effective learning exercise. The second program, "The Game of Life," demonstrates and teaches the basics of mouse control and selection, as well as providing one of the best versions of the game available.

With a little practice, the mouse is comfortable and easy to use. Within 30 minutes or so, you should find yourself using the mouse adeptly. And it really does speed up use of the program.

If you use a monochrome monitor, the mouse-controlled pointer appears on the *Word* screen as a blinking square of light. If you have a color/graphics board and a monitor that is capable of displaying graphics, however, the mouse pointer appears initially as an arrow at a 45-degree angle and changes shape, depending on the area of the screen it is in and the function it is performing. By moving the mouse across a table surface, *Word*'s pointer moves across the screen. By positioning the mouse, you can position the pointer wherever you want. By pressing the two mouse buttons singly or together, you can perform various text positioning and editing procedures.

The editing screen *Word*'s editing screen is where most editing, printing, and file-handling functions are executed. Unlike other programs that present a variety of menus from which to select options, *Word* presents a main menu—the command area—at the bottom of the editing screen. While the contents of *WordStar*'s main menu never changes, for example, the commands and messages at the bottom of the screen in *Word* vary according to the operation being performed.

The text-editing area of the screen can display 19 lines of text. It is enclosed in a rectangular box above the command area, and the lines surrounding the editing portion of the screen have special significance when they are used with the mouse. The text area is restricted to entering and editing text; to initiate commands and operations, you must move to the command area by moving the mouse or pressing the appropriate key.

Within the text area you may see three symbols: the selection indicator (much like the PC's standard cursor), a diamond marking the end of the document being edited, and the pointer (if you are using the mouse).

The borders of the *Word* screen are designed to take instructions from the mouse. The left and bottom borders of any screen window contain what the program calls "scroll bars." To scroll through a document vertically, you move the mouse pointer onto the left border. You click one button on the mouse to scroll up through a document, and the other mouse button scrolls text down. Moving the mouse pointer to the bottom screen border enables you to scroll left and right if the text exceeds the screen width.

Next to the vertical scroll bar on the left margin is a "selection bar." When the mouse pointer is in the selection bar, you can press a mouse button to select lines, paragraphs, or a whole document. For instance, to mark a paragraph for deletion, you can swing the mouse pointer left into the selection bar, position it beside the desired paragraph, and click a mouse button. Instantly, the entire paragraph is marked—without touching a key.

The upper and right borders of a screen or a window contain "window bars" for opening and closing windows. By moving the mouse pointer into either of these bars, you can press a button and divide the screen into smaller editing windows (up to a total of eight windows). With two windows, for example, you can display and compare two parts of the same document. The upper right corner of each screen has a "ruler button" for showing a ruler along the top of the screen. Although *Word* does not ordinarily display a ruler, by moving the pointer to the ruler button, you can press a mouse button and have the program display a ruler for reference during text formatting. The lower right corner of each screen has a "window move button," which enables you to adjust window size. Although you cannot see these "buttons" on the editing screen border, moving the pointer to them and clicking a button on the mouse activates their functions.

Features The command area occupies the bottom four lines of the screen. Displayed there are the menus and menu names, the message line for prompts and error messages, keyboard status codes that signal the condition of keys such as <CapsLock>, the document name, the percentage of memory remaining, and the contents of the "scrap." Any time you delete or copy information, text is held in the scrap (a buffer) until you get rid of it by copying more text into the scrap or making another deletion. The scrap is especially useful for restoring text that has been erased accidentally. *Word* shows you what is in the scrap between two braces at the bottom of the screen. If the amount of text is too large, only the beginning and the end of the text are shown, separated by an ellipsis.

Despite all the information on the editing screen, *Word* doesn't display the location of the cursor (its page, line, and column positions, for instance), which would be a useful feature. The program doesn't lack many other features, however. Cursor movement is quick and simple, although *Word* doesn't have a traditional cursor. You can position the pointer freely within a document using the mouse, and selecting text with the keyboard (without the mouse) is fast and easy. You can also move quickly to the beginning or the end of a document, or to a specific page.

Word has an excellent "Undo" feature. Choosing this command reverses the previous editing change. For example, if you deleted ten pages of text and wanted to restore them, the Undo command can make them instantly reappear. Undo is a handy editing feature for novices who are just getting used to word processing and who might be uneasy about making irreparable changes.

Although *Word* has a search and replace feature, you can't specify that the program search "n" number of times, as you can with some other programs. You can search for and replace words and phrases, and search for only uppercase or lowercase terms, or whole words. You can search forward or backward through a document and use wild-card characters and special characters in the search string that are not letters, numbers, or punctuation.

The help features of *Word* are almost too much of a good thing. There are extensive on-line, context-sensitive help screens, but you can get lost in layer upon layer of information. Given the poor state of the documentation, however, the help screens are a good supplement.

If you have a color/graphics board and graphics monitor, *Word* provides outstanding screen display of italics, boldface, small capitals, and other special type styles, including superscripts and subscripts. And special effects appear on the screen exactly as they will appear on paper. If you use the IBM Monochrome Display, however, the screen will display only underlining and boldface; the other type styles will all be represented by underlining, which can be confusing.

Word shines in the area of text formatting. You can select individual characters, paragraphs, or "divisions" for special formatting. Divisions are sections of text, such as paragraphs, pages, or larger portions of a document, that are formatted differently from surrounding text segments. Columnar information and lists that require specific formatting parameters are also good examples of divisions.

Word allows you to apply a set of formatting specifications to sections of selected text. For example, if you have just typed a 20-page document single-spaced and you want to have it double-spaced, select the whole document, give the command for double-spacing, and *Word* automatically double-spaces the whole text. You can center, indent, and justify text, and *Word* supports left, right, center, and decimal tabs. In fact, *Word* enables you to set tabs that automatically fill blank space between tabs with periods, hyphens, or underscoring. These features are not found in most other word processors available for the PC.

Although you can format text manually, *Word* has a "style sheet" feature that automates formatting. You can construct a detailed record, or style sheet, that defines the style of certain kinds of documents and controls the format of subsequent documents by assigning the style sheet to them (see Figure 5.1). If your business reports require formats that have specific line spacing, paragraph indentations, and margins, you can record these specifications in the style sheet. As you

```
1 C Heading a                                    CHARACTER
     BoldPS (roman a) 12 Uppercase. Centered.
2 D Other paragraph a                            DIALOGUE
     BoldPS (roman a) 12. Justified, Left indent 1.5", right indent 1.5",
     space after 1 li (keep in one column).
3 N Normal paragraph                             NARRATIVE (ACTION DESC.)
     BoldPS (roman a) 12. Justified, Left indent 0.75", right indent
     0.75", space after 1 li (keep in one column).
4 P Heading c                                    PARENTHETICAL
     BoldPS (roman a) 12. Flush right, right indent 3.17".
5 S Heading b                                    SHOT # & DESCRIPTION
     BoldPS (roman a) 12 Uppercase. Flush left, space after 1 li. Tabs
     at: 0.67" (left flush), 6.75" (right flush).
6   Normal division a
     Page break. Page length 11"; width 8.5". Folios Arabic. Top margin
     1"; bottom 1"; left 1"; right 1". Top running head at 0.5". Bottom
     running head at 0.5". Footnotes on same page.
```

Figure 5.1 *A style sheet that is used for formatting printed text with* Word.

type a report, the assigned style sheet automatically formats the report in the appropriate way. You can create style sheets for several different page layouts, titles, headings, lists, indexes, and special printing attributes. After creating a style sheet for the report document, you can then apply these same format specifications to other reports by pressing one or two keys. Using *Word* style sheets, you can give every document the same look automatically. You don't have to enter any formatting instructions when you produce documents—just call up the appropriate style sheet.

Style sheets are built and controlled through *Word*'s Gallery menu, and again the manual is not much help. But *Word*'s formatting is such a valuable aspect of the program that it shouldn't be overlooked or ignored just because it is difficult to learn.

Although most word processors have trouble producing footnotes, *Word* handles footnotes extraordinarily well. It can automatically number and print footnotes in the correct place, either on individual pages or at the end of a chapter. The program enables you to print columns of text on the pages to produce newspaper-style column formats. The program also provides automatic widow and orphan control. *Word* supports most of the popular dot matrix and letter quality printers.

Using the commands Most editing procedures are initiated with menu selections. Any command can be invoked using the keyboard or the mouse. *Word* does an excellent job of employing the function keys, and a keyboard template is supplied with the most recent version of the program.

Getting *Word* to do what you want involves selecting and executing commands. To select a command with the keyboard, you move the cursor to the desired command or type the first letter of the command. Commands often have several options or require you to answer "yes" or "no" to prompts. After setting the command options, you carry out the command by pressing <Enter>.

The mouse is by far the quickest way to navigate through the menus. To select a command using the mouse, put the pointer on the command, and press the left button. To execute the command, press the right button. The left mouse button selects, and the right one executes. It's that easy.

Word requires a minimum of 128K of memory and one disk drive. It can be loaded with a hard disk, and to take advantage of *Word*'s many special display capabilities, you can run it using a color/graphics board and a color or graphics monitor. Although only one disk drive is required, you can use the program more effectively with two drives. And although using a mouse requires an extra circuit board in the System Unit or a serial port, the efficiency in editing that the mouse provides over standard methods makes buying one worthwhile.

Word is one of the most sophisticated word processors available for the PC and the XT. Once adequate documentation is available to help you master its remarkable features, *Word* may well become the most popular word processor.

WordStar

Although *WordStar* is currently the most widely used word processing program for PC-standard computers, some people don't think it's the best one. Although MicroPro has corrected several earlier weaknesses in the latest version, 3.3, *WordStar* still lacks a number of features offered by newer word processors such as *Word*. *WordStar* is a reliable and flexible program, however, and it has the advantages of having a huge installed user base and a supporting body of literature.

Documentation *WordStar*'s documentation has improved greatly since the program first became available. The documentation is divided into three parts: the *Reference Manual;* the *Training Guide,* which offers three separate levels of instruction; and the *Installation Manual.*

The documentation is packaged in a three-ring, looseleaf binder. A welcome feature is a series of graphic symbols that alert readers to especially important material. The manual is written clearly and is well organized. It leads readers through various features and functions, and explains them adequately. Some attempt has been made to anticipate the mistakes readers are likely to make, and instructions for resolving those problems are included. The instructions tell you what keys to press, with the keys represented graphically, and then show you what should appear on the screen.

Features By the latest standards, *WordStar* might be considered lacking in features, but it does have the basic word processing features and a few others that even its latest competitors don't have.

WordStar has adequate cursor movement commands. You can use either the cursor keys on the numeric keypad or <Ctrl>-key combinations to direct the cursor around the screen. To move the cursor one character to the left using a <Ctrl>-key combination, you hold down the <Ctrl> key and type S. <Ctrl>-A moves the cursor one word to the left, <Ctrl>-D moves the cursor one character to the right, and <Ctrl>-F moves the cursor one word to the right. You can also move the cursor to the beginning or the end of a line or a document. You cannot, however, direct the cursor to a specific page.

WordStar scrolls using similar <Ctrl>-key sequences. <Ctrl>-W scrolls up one line, and <Ctrl>-Z scrolls down one line. To scroll up or down one screenful at a time, you can use either the <PgUp> and <PgDn> keys or a <Ctrl>-key combination.

To master moving the cursor and scrolling, you have to learn about ten commands, and then you will have only scratched the surface of *WordStar*'s command library. The program's critics are quick to cite the array of commands as one reason that the program is difficult to learn and use.

Like almost all programs, *WordStar* has automatic word wrap, which you can disengage if you wish. Although the program can move, copy, and delete blocks of text, it does not automatically reformat text during editing. Some would consider that inability a major disadvantage. After editing a paragraph, you have to move the cursor to the beginning of the paragraph and type <Ctrl>-B to reformat the text. You can automatically reformat an entire document with a similar command, but overall, *WordStar* requires an extra step for reformatting. And although you can delete a character, a word, or a line of text at a time, you cannot restore deleted text, because *WordStar* has no Undo feature.

WordStar has a nice "failsafe" feature, however. Whenever you save a document on disk, the program automatically makes a backup copy of the file.

Editing and formatting If you're looking for a program that provides editing windows, *WordStar* isn't for you. You cannot divide the *WordStar* editing screen.

It's difficult to write a program that meets the needs of both novices and experienced users, especially the level of help information displayed. Although novices usually appreciate as much help as they can get, once they attain some level of proficiency with the program, too much on-screen help becomes irritating. *WordStar* offers four levels of on-screen help and even lets you turn off the help feature completely.

Most users retain some of the basic on-screen information, which provides guidance for editing and formatting. At the top of the screen, for example, are cursor position indicators that show the page, the line, and the column position of the cursor in the document. The program also displays a ruler line that shows the document's left and right margins, and the position of tab stops. A good deal of the editing screen is used to display the primary command menu, which details the <Ctrl>-key combinations that perform many editing functions (see Figure 5.2). Users who have memorized the *WordStar* commands can suppress this menu, however, so that the entire screen is available for text. If the program is in Insert mode (its default mode), an "insert on" message appears at the top of the screen. At the bottom of the screen are labels showing the tasks assigned to the ten function keys.

Special printing attributes, such as boldface and under-

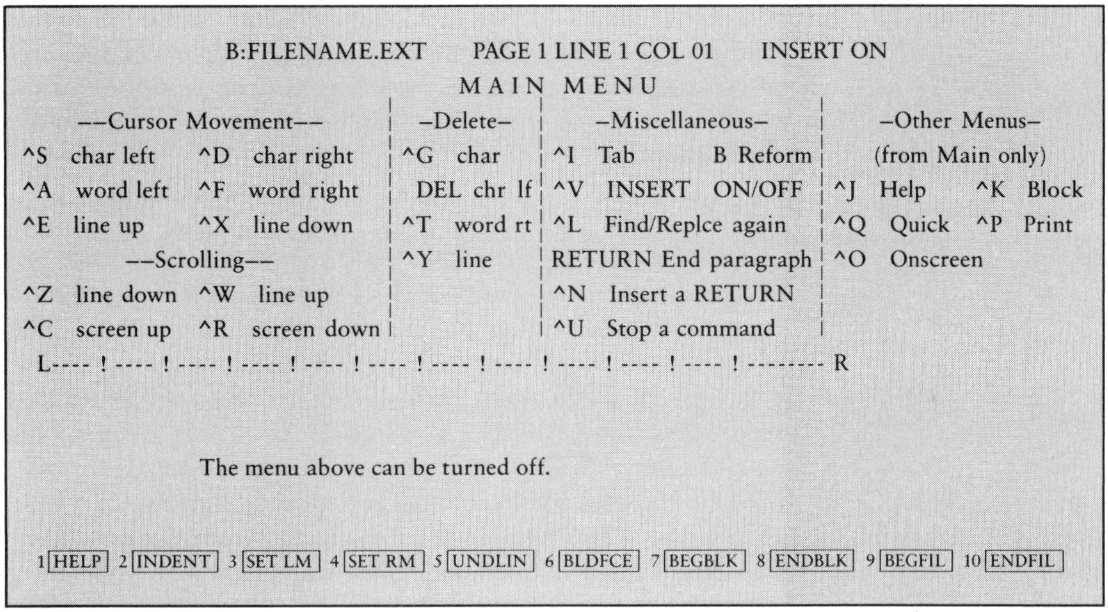

Figure 5.2 *The editing menu of* WordStar *showing the file name and cursor position, summary of commands (which can be turned off), text area, and function key commands.*

lining, are indicated by codes embedded in the text. For example, if you want to print the word *star* in boldface, you have to type <Ctrl>-PB before and after the word. What you see on the screen is ^Bstar^B. You have to type the boldface command twice, because it is a toggle switch. The first <Ctrl>-PB turns the toggle on, and the second one turns it off. If you don't enter the second command to turn it off, the rest of the document will be printed in boldface. *WordStar* uses embedded codes to perform boldface, underlining, strikeout, subscripts, and superscripts.

A number of *WordStar*'s formatting procedures require codes, called dot commands, that are embedded in the text. For example, the codes that set the top and bottom margins of a document at six lines are .MT 6 and .MB 6. (*WordStar*'s default margins are three lines at the top and eight lines at the bottom.) These codes send instructions to the printer, and although they appear on the screen, they do not print on paper. Except for these embedded codes, what you see on the screen is what you will get on paper.

WordStar's formatting features are standard except for justification. Although justification sometimes produces attractive text, it can present problems when you are trying to produce columns. Fortunately, the *WordStar* manual tells you how to avoid these problems. Although *WordStar* features full justification, it doesn't offer flush right or centered formatting, although individual lines can be centered after you have typed them.

WordStar 3.3 makes good use of the function keys: <F1> sets the level of help the program provides, <F5> inserts the underline code, <F6> inserts the boldface code in text at the cursor position, and <F9> and <F10> move the cursor to the beginning and the end of a file, respectively. The *Installation Manual* lists the assigned functions for the function keys. You can also assign almost any program commands to the function keys when you initially configure the program.

Many of *WordStar*'s features can be customized to suit the way the user works. Using the installation program, you can set the defaults for 19 features. Even better, if you decide that you want to change the default during editing, you can often do so with a command.

Related programs MicroPro produces several programs that work directly with *WordStar. CorrectStar* and *MailMerge* can run from the *WordStar* menu, and *StarIndex* runs independently of *WordStar.* All three programs are included in MicroPro's *WordStar Professional* package, but they can be purchased separately.

CorrectStar is a spelling checker that proofreads text and marks possible spelling errors. The main dictionary used by *CorrectStar* includes 65,000 words and is based on the *American Heritage Dictionary* from Houghton Mifflin. The documentation for *CorrectStar* is good and has the same style as *WordStar*'s. But the program itself is so easy to use that you won't need to refer to the guide often.

MailMerge performs three basic operations: entering variable information into a master document, such as several names and addresses in a form letter; chaining documents together for printing, such as the chapters of a book; and "nesting" information inside a document, such as standard passages in a contract or a legal document. For applications such as producing mass mailings, *MailMerge* demonstrates the processing power of the PC.

StarIndex works with *WordStar*-compatible files to create indexes, tables of contents, lists of figures, and lists of tables. It automates some of the more tedious tasks associated with producing long documents. The defaults in *StarIndex* can be changed to suit your needs. Once you have created a new format for an index or a table, you can save it and use it later.

WordStar is an excellent program in its own right. And used in conjunction with the other programs offered by MicroPro, it becomes the center of a useful office system. Although it lacks some of the newer word processing features, such as multiple editing windows, a mouse pointing device, and an Undo function, it is powerful, time tested, and reliable.

CHAPTER SIX

Data Base Management Systems

Data is the lifeblood of business, and nothing pumps out data better than a data base management system (DBMS). There is some confusion among many microcomputer users as to exactly what a DBMS is, because the term *data base* is sometimes used to refer to different things. This chapter examines some of the theory and the terminology of data base management systems and tells you how to use this powerful application to manage business information.

A data base is nothing more than a collection of information; its management system is the way the information is organized. You probably use some familiar manual data base management systems every day. Understanding the features of some of these systems is helpful for understanding their electronic counterparts. For example, a book with a table of contents and an index is a DBMS. A dictionary is a more specialized type of DBMS, and a library is an even more complex system.

In businesses, an accounting system is a highly specialized DBMS; in fact, accounting is a common application for microcomputer DBMS programs. Probably the most common data management system in business is the paper filing system, with its manila folders, labels, and file drawers. In the pages that follow, we will use the filing system example to illustrate some of the more basic data management concepts and terminology.

There are three basic types of electronic DBMSs: file managers, relational DBMSs (RDBMSs), and network or hierarchical data management systems. This chapter focuses on the types of systems that you will be most likely to need and use: file managers and relational data base management systems. Because they are used primarily with large computers, network DBMSs aren't covered in this book. Accounting systems are a specialized type of network DBMS and are covered later, in Chapters 12 and 13.

The basic elements of any data base are *files, records, fields,* and *keys.* A *file* is a collection of related information, such as a list of names, addresses, and telephone numbers or an inventory of products. You might consider a file as one drawer in a file cabinet.

For the most part, you will be working with two kinds of files: master and transaction. *Master files* can be thought of as standing files used mainly for reference purposes. A typical master file won't have many records added to it, but the contents of the file may need to be updated frequently. For example, a file of customers is a master file. You add a record only when you add a new customer, but you update the file to record customers' purchases of your products. Inventory and suppliers' files are also master files.

A typical *transaction file* can have many records added to it, but there is often little need to go back into the file to update earlier records. For example, a transaction file may chronicle business activities and is usually related to one or more other files. A file of sales of a product is a transaction file. This file is related to your customer file if you include information about which customer bought the product. Powerful data base managers use these kinds of relationships among files to offer fast and flexible access to a data base.

One can imagine an electronic file as a matrix of rows and columns, not unlike a spreadsheet. In a data base, each row in a file is called a *record,* and each column is called a *field* (see Figure 6.1). You might think of a record as analogous to one folder in a file cabinet.

A *field* is simply a component of a record. Each record usually has several fields. For instance, in a file of customers you might have a record for the Acme Company. Fields for Acme might include street address, city, state, zip code, number of products purchased during the prior year, number purchased for the year to date, and so on. Fields are pieces of information related to the overall record, analogous to the individual pieces of paper in a file folder.

At least one field in each record is specially designated for manipulating data. This field, called the *key,* is used to identify and compare records. For example, the key in a customer file might be the customer's name, and the key in an address list might be the zip code. The data base program searches, sorts, and compiles data by using the key field. Many programs accommodate several key fields. Thus, the key is a critical link in a data management system.

Figure 6.1 *A list of names and addresses in a typical data base format, arranged in zip code order. Each element between commas is a* field, *each complete line is a* record, *and all the lines make up a* file.

Mike, McGillicuddy, 23 Grove St., Taunton, MA, 02770, 617/456-7890

Cynthia, Pitt, 4 Quilt Lane, Ocalala, NY, 10303, 916/333-3333

Susan, Smith, 5 Oak St., Harrison, NY, 10389, 916/345-6789

Neil, Friend, 3345 Quaker Way, Fell, PA, 15898, 412/789-1234

Lawrence, Descanso, 90 Market St., Gold Creek, MD, 20789, 301/123-4567

Jennifer, Bader, 8909 1st St., Ames, IO, 52345, 319/890-1234

Eliza, Boyd, 2 Cepa Way, Midtown, IL, 60738, 312/234-5678

Jerusha, Clapp, 1714 Bourne St., Lava Springs, ID, 83456, 208/180-7000

Joseph, Katz, 77 Blaze Blvd., Clawston, UT, 84393, 801/123-4567

Manuel, Sanchez, 787 Post St., Sutter, CA, 97343, 408/456-7890

File Management Systems

A file management system (FMS) is the simplest type of DBMS. In fact, some people argue that the FMS is not a data base management system at all, because it doesn't have the structure and capabilities of some of the more sophisticated DBMSs. While this argument is probably technically correct, we will keep the concepts simple and consider the FMS as a simple type of DBMS.

The principal virtues of any FMS are simplicity and ease of use in recording and accessing information, although most file managers cannot handle complex data bases. The best uses for an FMS are simple, structured, well-defined tasks, such as managing information in a mailing list. Usually an FMS can handle only one file at a time, but some programs have multiple-file capabilities. The ability to work with only one file at a time is the primary characteristic that distinguishes a file management system from a relational DBMS.

Another limitation of an FMS is that you cannot perform a single operation on an entire file with one command. For example, you can't change the contents of a field in every record simultaneously. In practical terms, this means that a file manager's data is more difficult to update or change than the data in a relational DBMS. With an FMS, you have to make sure that you set up a data base correctly the first time, or face laborious restructuring later.

Another distinguishing characteristic of the file manager is that it rarely has a built-in programming language. Thus, you can't easily customize an FMS. The most powerful programming features are generally found in an RDBMS, not in an FMS.

Relational Data Base Management Systems

The RDBMS is extremely popular among personal computer users, and with good reason. It is a powerful and flexible tool for managing information that until recently was available only to mainframe computer users. RDBMSs have, however, a major drawback: they are seldom easy to use, and much of the available literature about relational data base managers is arcane, to say the least.

The terminology of an RDBMS sometimes differs from that of an FMS. Some relational data base programs, including *R:Base 4000* (Microrim), refer to a collection of organized data as a *relation,* rather than a file. Records are called *rows,* and fields are called *attributes*. For purposes of clarity, however, this text uses the more common terms *file, record,* and *field* throughout.

Complicated explanations are often given concerning the way a relational data base is structured and how it works inside a computer. To put it very simply, however, data is organized flexibly within a relational system. You don't have to be as precise in setting up the format of a data base as with an FMS, and, once it's set up, you can change it more easily than you can change a highly structured FMS.

With an RDBMS, you can actually form new data bases from all or part of your existing data, using the powerful relational commands. For example, you can combine two files to form a new third file, or take parts of two to form a third. Although the way an RDBMS works is actually far more complex, it seems as if data in a relational system is simply stored in one big pot, thus allowing it to be accessed, manipulated, and retrieved in just about any way.

Data Base Design

The first step in using a DBMS is to establish the design for a data base—for example, the number of fields and the maximum length of each. Next, you enter the data. Finally, you can retrieve data by querying the program and generating reports to be displayed on the screen or printed on paper.

Data base design is an important initial step in creating a data base, particularly with an FMS, in which the data base definitions are difficult to alter once they are established. There are two aspects to data base design: logical and physical. *Logical design* is the process of planning what type of data you need recorded and how you want to use it. *Physical design* is the process of implementing your logical design on the computer—designing and building the actual files.

Designing a data base is a task that, in part, makes using DBMS software difficult. You can't just load a DBMS program into the PC and merrily begin computing. You must first do some careful planning. And while you might think that logical design shouldn't be much more involved than designing a spreadsheet— think again. A business data base can be big and pervasive. It probably will cut across most aspects of your business, and you will likely use it every day and depend on it to keep the business running smoothly. The consequences of a poorly planned or inefficient DBMS can disastrously affect business activities.

In order to create a strong design, first formulate the key objective that you want the data base to help you accomplish. Put it in writing. Because you probably have several reasons for setting up a data base, state them explicitly. Note the elements you will need to meet your primary objectives. And decide what formats are best for retrieving and arranging information from the data base.

For example, if you decide to create a data base to keep track of business expenses, your objectives might include making tax calculation easier and providing guidelines for budget planning in future years. The elements of such a data base (the fields in each record) might include the type of expense, amount, dates of transaction, whether it can be expensed or depreciated, and so on. Once the format for entering data is designed, you can devise one or more reports to be compiled from the data base, such as total business expenses, the total for each category of expense, and the total for a given month or other time period.

But if the data base is complex, the design process can become unwieldy and confusing. To simplify things, draw a flow chart of the data base, a simple depiction of the various data base elements and how they might fit together. The process of charting a data base often helps to clarify the structure and reveal omissions.

Data Entry

Once the design of the data base is complete, there is still one more chore: the data entry process of building files and their composite records, fields, and so forth. Data entry is often a procedure similar to filling in the blanks on a form, and usually the same screens that are used to enter data are also used for editing. When you are ready to enter your data, the program displays a screen format on which you enter the contents of one record. If you are entering data for the first time, blank space appears where each field can be filled in, and you will be prompted to enter the required data. If you are editing, the contents of the record are displayed, and you can make necessary changes or deletions.

An RDBMS offers considerable flexibility in entering and editing data. It provides a form design feature that enables you to design your own on-screen format for data entry. You can arrange the data entry format to look like a letter, a graph, or a table, for example. Fields can be logically combined; for example, an area code and phone number displayed together. You can also clarify your data entry screens with messages or instructions, and the same forms can be used for retrieving and editing data.

A requirement for data entry for both simple and sophisticated data base programs is precision. If you don't conform to the rules that you established when you defined the fields, the program will not accept your input. For example, entering letters in a field that requires numbers might create an invalid record. The better programs give clear error messages when you make a mistake and also tell you how to correct the error.

DBMS Features

One of the most powerful features of an RDBMS is its ability to edit any or all fields with single, far-reaching commands. For instance, if the U.S. Postal Service were to implement the nine-digit zip code, you could, with one command, change the format for every five-digit zip code in your data base to accommodate nine digits. You can also add or change fields throughout a file by using mathematical operators. For example, suppose you have a large employee file, and in each employee's record is a field listing that person's salary; you want to add a 10 percent adjustment for inflation to each employee's salary. Using a relational data base, with one command you could multiply every salary in the entire data base by 1.1, a feat that is impossible using a simple file management program.

All this data design and entry is defined and summarized by a common feature of advanced RDBMSs, the *data dictionary*. The dictionary includes such items as a definition of your data base records and fields, rules for data validation, a list of key fields, and passwords for restricting access to part or all of the data base. You might think of the data dictionary as a blueprint used in the construction of a data base edifice.

Another feature of an advanced DBMS is the ability to create menus. Menus can simplify using a program by allowing the user to execute complex sequences of commands by making simple choices from menu options. Menus not only save keystrokes for the experienced user but also enable inexperienced users to use data base managers effectively.

Some sophisticated DBMS programs enable you to program into them the features you require. Such programs, notably *dBASE II* (Ashton-Tate), include a comprehensive language that can be used to write other sophisticated data management programs. In fact, Ashton-Tate's file manager *Friday!* is written in the *dBASE II* language.

Don't be too concerned with programming an RDBMS; it is a task better left to a skilled computer programmer. In fact, a number of commercially available computer programs take advantage of *dBASE II*'s programming capabilities to make it easier to use, or to extend its power. One such program, *Quickcode* (Fox & Geller), is known as a program generator. This type of program can produce data management programs using *dBASE II* code to perform a variety of simple but special applications. Although it does not require any programming expertise, you will need to understand data management in some depth to get the most out of *Quickcode* and similar programs. Another program extender for *dBASE II*, *dGRAPH* (Fox & Geller), gives you the ability to create graphics with *dBASE II*.

Retrieving and Manipulating Data

Once you have designed your data base and have entered the data, you can retrieve the data in a variety of ways. This phase of electronic data management is a large part of the reason why many people consider data base programs so difficult to use.

Retrieving data from a DBMS is usually called *data query*. A basic file manager enables you to call up records and sort them alphabetically, numerically, or by other specified indexes. Any FMS program will give fast access to data when you request a sort by the key field, but when you sort by multiple fields, as many programs can do, the processing time required can be long.

The best RDBMSs have powerful data query features that allow you to manipulate as well as retrieve data. You can retrieve one or all fields by name, specify which records you want using up to ten conditional statements, sort the selected records, request numerical totals for each field, and compute functions such as sum, average, maximum, or minimum for any given field.

Closely linked to data query is the report function of a DBMS. Obviously, whatever the complexity of a program's data query features, the report writer should generate equally complex reports. Top-of-the-line programs display reports on screen, print them, and enable you to record them on disk as files. Some programs have powerful built-in report writers, and others treat advanced report generators as an option that can be purchased separately.

With a sophisticated program, you can create reports that have titles, summaries, labels, and varied formats. Your reports can be formatted as text, tables, graphs, and so on. One nice feature is the ability to do computations, such as calculating the average and maximum values of specific data totals. Printed reports can also usually include special messages and characters.

The report-writing capabilities of a program are closely linked to its forms features. If you can create elaborate on-screen forms for entering data, you can usually use the same formatting features for retrieving and printing data.

Data Base Applications

Data management is so pervasive in the business world that applications of data base technology are extensive. What might not be obvious is that many apparently different types of computer programs are actually just specialized data base managers. For example, a mailing list program is a DBMS, and interactive accounting system software is an example of a highly structured network DBMS.

The PC is a godsend for small and medium-sized businesses when it comes to managing data. The newest relational programs have both the power and the capacity to manage an entire data base for smaller businesses. And you don't necessarily need programming skills to use these programs effectively.

Very large businesses are still the province of mainframe-based data management systems serviced by data processing departments. But the PC or the XT and advanced DBMS software are an ideal combination for managing parts of a larger data base. You could retrieve data from your company's mainframe into your PC and maintain your own data base for quick reference and analysis.

Common areas for applying data management software include inventory management, sales and marketing, personnel, finance, strategic planning, and accounting. Every organization, including nonprofit operations such as universities and hospitals, can find applications for electronic filing. And the simplest file management programs are also useful for home applications.

The next chapter examines a basic FMS, *pfs:file* and *pfs:report,* and a powerful RDBMS, *R:base 4000*. Some of the features of *dBASE II,* one of the most popular first-generation relational programs for the IBM PC and XT, are also discussed.

CHAPTER SEVEN

An Introduction to pfs:file and pfs:report, dBASE II, and R:base 4000

The capabilities of microcomputer data base management systems run the gamut from simple file management programs to sophisticated relational or network systems. For several years the most sophisticated data base manager has been *dBASE II* (Ashton-Tate). It has been so popular that many secondary programs have been developed to support and enhance its capabilities. These program generators and enhancement programs enable you to add functions such as graphics or statistical analysis. This chapter covers both *dBASE II* and *Quickcode* (Fox & Geller), a program that makes *dBASE II* easier to use.

Although it is popular, *dBASE II* has won no awards for ease of use. To run the program, you often have to enter long strings of commands using a strict and complex command order, or syntax. Other programs with comparable power are easier to use. One of these, *R:base 4000* (Microrim), is covered in this chapter. To provide a counterpoint to these powerhouse systems, the chapter begins with a basic data manager, *pfs:file* (Software Publishing), and its companion program, *pfs:report*.

pfs:file and pfs:report

pfs:file is a simple file management program that enables you to create your own data entry forms on screen, enter data into them, store the data in individual files, and retrieve the data. When retrieving information, you have several options, such as finding information based on numeric matches and exact character (spelling) matches. Although *pfs:file* prints the results of its data retrievals, it cannot print organized reports using the information retrieved.

To create professional reports with *pfs:file* data, you have to use *pfs:report.* This program is specifically designed to work with *pfs:file;* it uses the data files produced by *pfs:file* to create tabular formatted reports. The program can also perform basic sorts and numerical calculations on the data.

Documentation The manuals for *pfs:file* and *pfs:report* are direct and concise, but they do not include separate tutorials illustrating the features of the programs. Instead, after each major section of the manual, examples and sample data are used to illustrate major program functions. The *pfs:file* manual first uses a sample file throughout the manual to provide examples of the program's operation. With a larger, more complex program, this method would not be effective, but with *pfs:file* it works just fine.

Unlike *pfs:file, pfs:report* provides a sample file on the program disk that you then transfer to a blank disk to run the examples in the manual. The *pfs:report* manual has one major flaw: it fails to advise users that *pfs:report* must have a blank, formatted disk in drive B to use as a working disk for sorting. The only clues in the whole manual are a cryptic reference to "a blank, formatted diskette to use when sorting," with no mention of how or where to use it, and a belated explanation in an Appendix. This is a serious problem in a program designed for those with limited computer experience.

Both manuals are clearly written, well organized, and complete (with the one notable exception). The spiral binding enables you to lay the guides flat on your desk while you work. Although the illustrations are adequate, the indexes are not thorough.

Features *pfs:file* and *pfs:report* provide the bread-and-butter features of file management. Neither program offers surprising capabilities or slick options. Together, however, they are capable of providing effective data management on a small scale.

Using *pfs:file,* you can design your own data entry form. Each page can have up to 100 items (see Figure 7.1); forms can be up to 32 pages long. The first item in a form is designated as a key field, and the program retrieves data most quickly when the key is the first retrieval specification.

To enter data you simply move the cursor from item to item on the form and fill in the blanks. You can use function keys to enter the date or the time, and you can print a form any time it is on the screen. The program has a routine for saving the design of a single form, several selected forms, or a whole file of forms on disk, separately from the data you supply. You can also split a file and save part of it on another disk and merge files. Splitting and merging files with *pfs:file* are rather mechanical and cumbersome procedures, however, compared with similar operations on a relational data base management program.

Figure 7.1 *A sample data entry form for* pfs:file. *The information below the dotted line is status information provided by the program.*

```
Employee #:                              Hired:
Name:
Address:
City:                          State:              Zip:

Dept:                          Phone Ext:
Job Title:
Monthly Salary:

----------------------------------------------------------

File: STAFF                    DESIGN                   Page 1
F5-Date        F6-Time                                  F10-Continue
```

pfs:file can retrieve data by matching complete records or partial records, such as last names; by comparing numbers, using operators such as "less than," "greater than," or ranges of numbers; and by selecting items that don't match specific criteria. You can "browse" (review) the data you've entered and update it. You can also print all or part of a record, and the program will sort the data on one field, in either alphabetical or numerical ascending order.

Although you can easily delete individual records or all records from a file, changing the design of a record (a form) is difficult, if not impossible, if data has already been entered into the data base file. If no data has been entered, the form can be restructured easily. But if data has been entered, the program warns that reorganizing your files can take hours, if it can be done at all. This rigidity in form structure is one of the drawbacks of a file management system compared to a relational data base manager.

pfs:report prints reports in tabular form, and each report format can have up to 16 columns of data. The program can sort alphabetically or numerically using a single field, and any field can be designated as the first one for this purpose. For columns holding numeric data, you can total, count, or average the entries, and generate subtotals, subcounts, or subaverages whenever the item in column 1 changes.

pfs:report can produce up to three derived columns—ones that take their information from data in other columns. For example, column 2 in a report might be defined as the entry in column 1 plus 5. This is a handy option for producing derived figures such as bonuses, raises, inflation adjustments, and price increases (see Figure 7.2).

You can identify certain information with key words, and retrieve and sort using these keys. If you don't want the headings you have defined in a form to appear as column headings in a report, you can specify different headings. The program also has a function for storing up to eight predefined reports that you use routinely.

As the foregoing summary indicates, both *pfs:file* and *pfs:report* have a full complement of basic features. The programs are designed for individuals or businesses that have limited demands for organizing, retrieving, and displaying information.

Employee Bonus Report

Name	Job Title	Salary/Mo.	13% Bonus	Total Pay
Bennet, Liza	Secretary	1,200	156.00	1,356.00
Calvin, Curt	Process Engineer	3,600	468.00	4,068.00
Fawley, Susan	Engineering Associate	2,100	273.00	2,373.00
Peters, Marvin	Technician	1,100	143.00	1,243.00
Sanchez, Enrico	Design Engineer	3,250	422.50	3,672.50
Thomson, John	Company President	5,000	650.00	5,650.00
Woodhouse, Emma	Purchasing Manager	3,200	416.00	3,616.00
Woolf, James	Personnel Clerk	1,000	130.00	1,130.00
		Average:	332.31	2,888.56
		Total:	2,658.50	23,108.50

Figure 7.2 *A sample report created with* pfs:report.

pfs:file is menu-driven and uses a minimum of prompts and on-screen messages. *pfs:report* has a similar operating structure, and once you have worked with *pfs:file,* you can learn *pfs:report* quickly. Neither program provides a help function when you have a procedural question, however. You have to rely on error messages to get you out of trouble with the *pfs:* programs.

The *pfs:file* menus are sparse on information (see Figure 7.3). The same is true for the screens you use to enter and edit data. For instance, because the screen for designing a form has no borders or ruler, you don't know the boundaries of the work area. You also have to guess how much space is available for an entry when you are entering data.

Both *pfs:file* and *pfs:report* make good use of the PC function keys, but the <F10> key might cause some people problems. Instead of using <Enter> to initiate a command, the programs use <F10>. If you are used to using <Enter>, such a nonstandard command entry as this one will take some getting used to.

Once you have designed your form, you use that format to enter and retrieve data, and print reports with *pfs:report.*

PFS: FILE FUNCTION MENU

1 DESIGN FILE   5 PRINT
2 ADD   6 REMOVE
3 COPY   7 EXIT PFS:FILE
4 SEARCH/UPDATE

SELECTION NUMBER: _
FILE NAME:

(C) 1983 Software Publishing Corporation
F10-Continue

Figure 7.3 *The main menu of* pfs:file.

As you are editing or entering data in a form, you can return to the main menu quickly by pressing the <Esc> key, but whatever data you have entered will be lost if you haven't saved it. The manual alerts you to this problem with prominent warnings.

Neither program is particularly fast, especially when sorting or retrieving data on specifications other than the key item. *pfs:file*'s sorting speed, however, is comparable to other file managers.

Support To get support for your *pfs:* programs, you have to send in the User Group Enrollment Card provided in the manual. Software Publishing warrants each program for 90 days after purchase and will give you a new program disk if you have any problems during that period. The company also promises to notify users of any program updates. Program support would be better if the company added a toll-free phone number for customer service or included the technical support phone number in the manuals.

Neither program has unusual hardware requirements. You can run either program on a PC that has 64K of RAM and one disk drive, although two drives are recommended.

pfs:file and *pfs:report* are the Volkswagens of the data management world. Although they offer no frills, they are priced low and are easy to use. The next program is more like a Porsche—powerful and sophisticated but a handful to use.

dBASE II

dBASE II (Ashton-Tate) is unfriendly to newcomers. While complaints about the program's capabilities have been few, many people have criticized it for having poor documentation and being difficult to use. Yet you can find articles that praise it for ease of use, even for beginners.

Why the discrepancy? The problem seems to be one of perception. *dBASE II* is actually two programs in one. It's a relational data base manager that has good basic features, which can be used for simple file management applications without too much difficulty. For someone who has never used one of the newest relational systems or one of the more powerful file management systems, *dBASE II* may be a good choice for simple jobs—if you can afford to ignore the more powerful (and difficult to learn) features.

dBASE II is also a powerful program development system with its own programming language. People who have had lots of experience using computers and data base management programs appreciate its many features and flexibility in data processing and tend to underestimate its difficulty for less experienced microcomputer users. Although the most recent versions of *dBASE II* acknowledge the needs of first-time users, the program is definitely not easy to use.

Recently Ashton-Tate released an enhanced DBMS program, *dBASE III*. It has been made faster and more powerful than *dBASE II*, and it contains a variety of menus and on-screen help messages designed to make the program easier to use than *dBASE II*.

Documentation From the beginning, the *dBASE II* documentation is confusing, badly organized, overly technical, and poorly written. To make any sense of the installation instructions, for example, you have to refer to other parts of the manual. The program does include a tutorial on three disks, however, which makes up for many of the manual's deficiencies. Although a pocket-sized quick-reference card is included, you can't really use it unless you already know how to operate the program.

Features *dBASE II* has most of the features any user would want in a relational system. It can accommodate up to 65,535 records per file, 1000 characters per record, 32 fields per record, and 254 characters per field. Although other programs have larger data capacities, *dBASE II* is adequate for most users' requirements.

dBASE II enables you to create a data base system that specifically reflects a business's information storage and retrieval needs. You can process data using logical operators such as "And," "Or," and "Not," and arithmetic operators that perform addition, subtraction, division, and multiplication. Information can also be processed using relational operators that allow comparisons such as less than, greater than, equal to, not equal to, less than or equal to, and greater than or equal to. Although these operators may not mean much to the novice data base user, they enable you to search for, sort, and retrieve data in flexible and efficient ways.

The program provides about 15 functions and more than 100 commands that can be used to customize the data base management. You can devise special menus, create and manipulate several data base files at once, split and join files, derive new data bases from previously created files, and add, edit, delete, display, and print data using these commands. Although mastering *dBASE II*'s programming language requires considerable savvy, the many commands, operators, and functions enable experienced users to adapt *dBASE II* to a wide range of applications.

Independent programmers have adapted this program for many uses. The *dBASE II* documentation lists a variety of customized applications developed by outside companies for such activities as engineering, financial analysis, insurance, hotel services, mailing lists, medical and dental services, club memberships, property management, publication and subscription management, sales and inventory management, and accounting. Whether the interest is in dairy farm management or stock portfolio analysis, *dBASE II* can usually provide the information processing capabilities required by microcomputer users.

A novice may not get far, however, if he or she plans to open the manual and start programming custom applications with *dBASE II*. Like any specialized programming, it requires the mastery of many commands to create even a simple menu of choices for an application. The average business user who simply wants to do the work and is not interested in programming may be better off choosing one of the ready-made applications of *dBASE II* or using the program with one or more enhancement programs that simplify its operation.

Quickcode Fortunately, many programs are designed to take the pain out of using *dBASE II*. One such program is *Quickcode* (Fox & Geller), a program generator that operates with *dBASE II*. With minimum effort on your part, it will automatically produce program modules or a complete data base management system, including menus in the *dBASE II* language.

The *Quickcode* documentation provides a brief introduction to and overview of the program, then detailed installation instructions. Two chapters are devoted to getting *Quickcode* started, using the main menu, generating programs using the programs that you create, and presenting a sample mailing list program. The second half of the documentation serves as a reference for experienced users, detailing how *Quickcode* works and explaining the program modules it produces. The documentation ends with a discussion of new features added to the latest *Quickcode* version, and appendices list common programming problems, the use of ASCII characters, and special *Quickcode* features. The manual is well organized and well written.

Quickcode is much easier to use than its host program, *dBASE II*. You design a *Quickcode* program by working with three basic screens. On the first screen, you design a data entry and retrieval form; on the second you define all the elements of your data dictionary, or the types and lengths of data you will be recording; and on the third you choose the type of program you want to create. *Quickcode* offers a choice of 12 program types, and because the programs are written in *dBASE* code, they can be modified to suit individual data processing needs.

For people who already have *dBASE II*, *Quickcode* is a valuable program development tool. For beginners, *Quickcode* can simplify the effort required to get a basic data base system up and running with *dBASE II*. *Quickcode* is also a handy tool for programmers who are making large data base management systems, because it can quickly create the many standard modules that any system needs, freeing the programmers to work on the more specialized parts of the system.

R:base 4000

R:base 4000 (Microrim) demonstrates that sophisticated relational data base management systems for the PC and the XT don't have to be difficult to use. This program has advanced features and implements them in an easy-to-understand manner that makes the program a pleasure to use. And the documentation and support are also outstanding.

Documentation *R:base 4000* comes in a clothbound three-ring binder that contains the manual, two program disks, a tutorial disk, a tutorial guide, and a summary of the program's commands. These elements represent excellent examples of documentation. The materials are first rate—typeset and with plenty of screen illustrations—and the writing is well organized and clear, with a minimum of jargon. The table of contents, the glossary, and the index are thorough and well organized.

Features *R:base 4000* has many special features as well as all the standard features of a relational system. The standard features include a data dictionary for defining fields and records, a data input module, a data editing section, a data query module for retrieving data in a variety of ways, a report writer, and a module for sharing data with other applications programs. This program also has five powerful relational commands that enable you to create new data bases from existing ones. Finally, *R:base 4000* has a security feature that enables you to restrict access to specific information as well as to an entire data base.

R:base 4000 has an excellent data entry module. For example, you can create customized data entry forms and use the same forms for retrieving and editing data. You can also load data from a disk file directly into a form. The program takes full advantage of the PC's ability to create striking graphic effects with special characters.

The program provides excellent flexibility in searching for information stored in a data base. You can retrieve data using up to ten conditional statements, such as equals, not equals, greater than, and less than. The program sorts in ascending or descending order, based on up to ten fields. *R:base 4000* also computes on selected fields, including functions such as count, average, sum, minimum, and maximum.

R:base 4000 includes a good report writer. Because all the design capabilities of the custom form function can be accessed by the report writer, you can add headings and other details to your reports. If your requirements exceed the capabilities of the standard report writer, Microrim offers an *Extended Report Writer* for the program.

The capacities of *R:base 4000* are impressive. You can have up to 40 separate files in one data base. Within each file, you can have up to 2.5 billion individual records (if your computer has adequate storage for that much data). The maximum length of any one record is 1530 characters. *R:base 4000* is clearly a program that can handle the bigger jobs.

Information in the program's data bases can be transferred to other popular applications programs, including *Multiplan, VisiCalc, 1-2-3, dBASE II,* and *WordStar. R:base 4000* can also be customized to provide files that contain series of commands or specialized menus.

The program's command language is concise and simple to use. Although it is command-driven, extensive on-screen assistance is available when you are using the commands. If you can't remember exactly how to use a certain command, typing "prompt" followed by a command displays on-screen "fill-in-the-blank" procedures to carry out the command (see Figure 7.4). If you just need information, you can type "help" and view a listing of all the program's commands (see Figure 7.5), or you can type "help" followed by a command name to get specific help information. The program employs extensive on-screen prompts throughout to help you move smoothly through the functions, and the error messages are excellent.

The on-screen prompts are so extensive that you could almost run the program without reading the documentation. And the on-line tutorial enables you to learn the program without painstakingly studying the manual. Novices can use *R:base 4000* for simple applications right away and learn to use the more advanced capabilities later, as the needs of their business applications grow. Microrim has obviously thought

Push [ESC] when done with this data

DEFINE

The DEFINE command enters the define mode where you can set up a new database or add to the definition of an existing one. You must first define a database name and drive, then you can create attributes, relations, and optionally, passwords and rules for your database. You can also define an owner password for the new database. Database names are from one to seven characters and can be prefaced by a drive indicator, i.e., B:ABC.

PROMPTS

Remember to include the drive before the database name (i.e., B:dbname).
Database name: _
Owner password:

Figure 7.4 *An example of the on-line help messages provided in* R:base 4000. *A comparable explanation is provided for each major command in the program.*

carefully about who will be using the program.

R:base 4000 has a 30-day warranty and a customer support hot line (not a toll-free number).

The program requires a PC or an XT with 256K of RAM, two disk drives (one can be a hard disk), and PC-DOS 1.10 or higher. Considering the program's data-handling capacities, the increased storage capacity of a hard disk drive seems appropriate to take full advantage of *R:base 4000*.

HELP

R:base is a relational database management system. A database is a collection of tables (called relations) that you can define, load with data, query, and modify using the following:

ASSIGN	EDIT	INTERSECT	OUTPUT	RENAME	SUBTRACT
ATTRIBUTES	END	JOIN	PASSWORDS	REPORTS	TALLY
BUILD	ENTER	LISTATT	PRINT	RULES	UNION
CHANGE	EXIT	LISTREL	PROJECT	SELECT	UNLOAD
COMPUTE	FORMS	LOAD	RELOAD	SET	WHERE
DEFINE	HELP	NEWPAGE	RELATIONS	SHOW	
DELETE	INPUT	OPEN	REMOVE	SORT	

To guide yourself using the screen command prompting feature enter PROMPT.
To return to this list of commands enter HELP.

SYNTAX

Use this syntax for the HELP command:
HELP (command)
Within the HELP module you do not need to preface commands with the word "HELP".

Enter the keyword for the help text you want or END to leave the help module.

H> □

Figure 7.5 *The menu of on-line help provided in* R:base 4000.

CHAPTER EIGHT

Business Graphics

Although some writers might not agree that a picture is worth a thousand words, few would argue that a picture is worth a thousand numbers. Graphics can convey trends and relationships in a complicated series of numbers more vividly than can the numbers alone.

Business graphics are sometimes confused with the general category of computer graphics—images created with the computer to inform, entertain, or just dazzle the eye. But in business graphics, the primary emphasis is on the generation of charts and graphs to represent complex numerical business data. With business graphics programs, you can produce a variety of charts and graphs on your computer screen and print or plot them on paper, ready to be used in presentations, speeches, or reports.

Business graphics are becoming a popular application for the PC and the XT, and with good reason. The traditional way of creating business graphics is to approach an artist with a rough sketch of a chart and as much additional information as possible about the necessary characteristics, such as scale, titles, and legends. The process is often hit or miss, and occasionally the artist will not be able to capture the right meaning or nuance. And getting a chart done often takes a long time, which can be a problem if you are under the pressure of a deadline. The process of producing graphics is expensive, whether the artist works in-house or as an independent contractor.

With business graphics programs, you can generate your own graphics in minutes, designed just the way you want them, and at a fraction of the cost of graphics produced by hand. And if you decide that you don't like the chart you have created, you can revise it in seconds.

Computer-generated graphics involve some compromises, however. Most business graphics programs on the market today cannot produce work of quality comparable to that of a graphic artist. In fact, some programs produce graphics that look primitive if you are used to seeing top-notch work. Pie charts tend to be not quite round, layouts may be stark, and line quality can be faint.

Most business graphics programs require special hardware. You need a printer that can produce graphics and is compatible with your program, and you will need a color printer or plotter if you want to produce color charts. Your computer must have an IBM Color/Graphics Adapter or a similar graphics board to produce graphics on a color monitor or a graphics-capable monochrome monitor. The IBM graphics adapter does not work with the IBM Monochrome Display, which can't display graphics without a special adapter, such as the Hercules Graphics Card (Hercules).

Although business graphics look spectacular on a color monitor, the poor resolution of text and numbers on a color monitor can cause eyestrain when the monitor is used for such applications as word processing or spreadsheets. If you plan to use different kinds of applications, you should consider buying both a monochrome and a color monitor. None of these hardware considerations should be final deterrents to incorporating business graphics programs into your software library, but you should be aware of them if you are considering business graphics software.

Producing Business Graphics

Most business graphics programs produce graphics in four phases: data entry and definition, chart specification, chart formatting, and output (saving and printing or plotting a chart). Some programs also offer time series analysis (discussed later in this chapter) for performing statistical analysis and forecasting. Most programs also have limited text-handling capabilities and some calculation functions.

Defining and entering data Data entry and definition with a business graphics program is similar to entering data in a data base management program. The data you enter represents the facts the chart will be based on. There are specific rules for the types of data that can be entered and how long each entry can be. If you enter the wrong type of data or enter it incorrectly, the program can't accept it and may display an error message or a prompt asking you to reenter the data correctly.

One rule of data entry with most business graphics programs is that data is always entered in pairs. By the very nature of plotting data on horizontal (*X*) and vertical (*Y*) axes, the program requires pairs of data to define locations on the chart or graph. Usually, the values plotted on the *X*-axis are some type of time-related data, such as a year, and the data for the *Y*-axis represents business values, such as sales or costs.

Some programs will automatically enter independent (time-related) values for you. All you need to do, when you begin entering data, is specify the starting date for your time series and the period of time between each entry. The default settings for these specifications in most programs are yearly entries with an increment of one year. If you enter 1983 for the first data pair, for example, the next entry would automatically be 1984. You can, of course, change the time interval to any length you want.

Many of these programs can accept data produced by other programs. If your data is already stored in the proper format on a disk, you can load it directly into the graphics program without having to enter it item by item. For example, *VisiCalc* data in DIF format can be used by many graphics programs, and some will accept data from other specific spreadsheet programs.

Along with the ability to enter new data, you can edit and update existing data in the data entry and definition phase. You can correct misspellings made while entering data, delete existing data, insert new entries, change the specifications originally set for the data series, or change the format in which the data is displayed.

Specifying chart types Defining the characteristics of a chart and producing it are fairly simple tasks for most business graphics programs. Almost all of them are menu-driven, with the notable exception of *BPS Business Graphics,* which is introduced in the next chapter.

After loading the data, you select the type of chart you want to create. There are essentially four types of charts: bar, line, pie, and scatterplot, or *X,Y* (see Figure 8.1). These four types can be combined or enhanced in various ways to create other types of charts. For example, an area chart is actually a line chart with the area below the line shaded in. A special variant of the scatterplot is the high-low-close chart, which shows the highest, lowest, and closing prices for a given stock.

Bar charts can be oriented vertically or horizontally, depending on program capabilities, and sometimes they can be displayed as if they have three dimensions. Bar charts can also

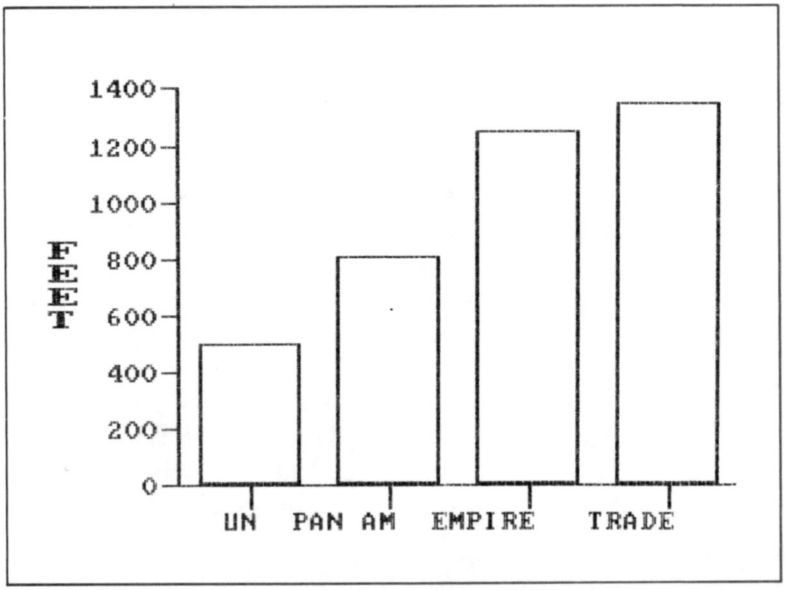

Figure 8.1 *Four sample charts generated from the same information. The charts shown are bar, line, pie, and scatterplot (following pages).*

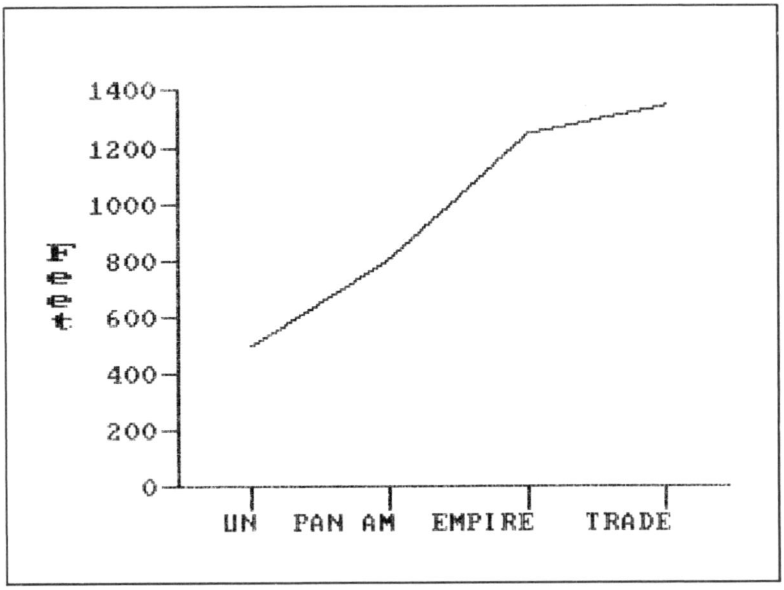
1400
1200
1000
800
600
400
200
0
Feet
UN
PAN AM
EMPIRE
TRADE

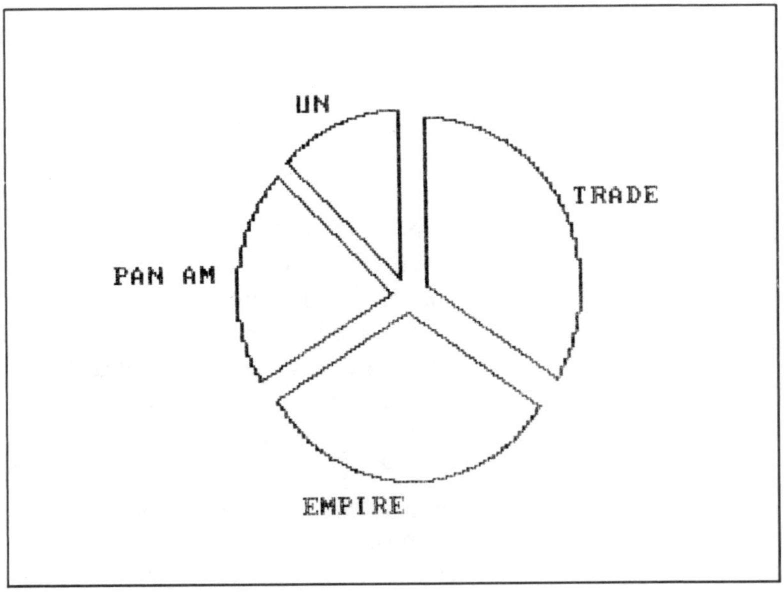
UN
TRADE
PAN AM
EMPIRE

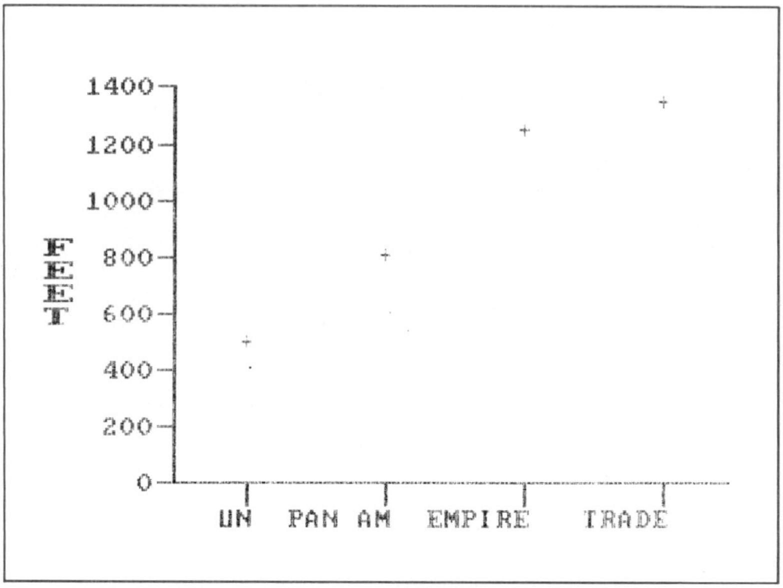

be stacked one on top of another, differentiated by varying colors or patterns. Pie charts can be displayed in a three-dimensional fashion as well, and a special variation called the exploded pie chart takes one "slice" of the pie, separates it from the rest of the chart, and enlarges and highlights it.

Most business graphics programs can combine and overlay charts in various ways (see Figure 8.2). For example, bar charts are frequently shown with line charts superimposed on top of the bars, and pie charts are also combined with bar charts to convey different aspects of the same data. Most programs can also display more than one chart on the same page, either side by side or stacked. Each type of chart is discussed in more detail, including suggestions for when to use each type, later in this chapter.

Once you have chosen the type of chart you want, the program creates the basic graph. The program automatically produces the proper range and scale for the chart, a process that can be very time-consuming if it is done manually.

The *range* of a chart defines the limits of the horizontal, or X-axis. For each data pair that you enter, the first value in each pair falls within the chart's range. For example, if you entered the sales figures for your company for each year from 1960 to 1984, the range of the chart would be 1960 to 1984.

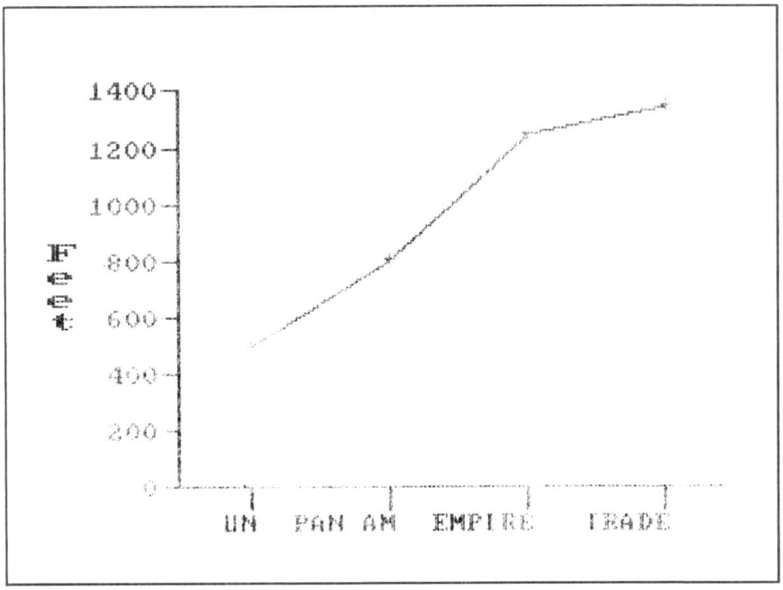

Figure 8.2 *An example of combining line and scatterplot charts.*

Although the program will automatically create the range on the *X*-axis, you can override the computer's choice if you want to. Also, if the range has too many values to fit on the axis, the program will abbreviate divisions between the numbers so they will all fit.

The *scale* of a chart is the spread of values plotted along the vertical, or *Y*-axis. Business graphics programs provide automatic scaling by setting up what appear to be natural divisions between the minimum and maximum data points entered. Most of the time the program will produce an appropriately scaled chart, but sometimes the scaling might be awkward, depending on the data used.

Although you can override the automatic scaling and choose your own scale, be careful when determining scale. Because range and scale are so closely related, if you change one, the other may have to be adjusted accordingly. Sometimes the program will automatically adjust range and scale, and sometimes it won't. Be sure you know how a particular program handles this situation before making adjustments of range or scale.

You can also use range and scale changes to highlight patterns in a data series that might not be apparent with an automatically scaled chart. For example, by compressing the range and the scale, you can highlight small variations in the data that might be especially important.

After you have created a chart on the screen, you might decide that the data could be communicated better with a different kind of chart. Since you already have the data loaded, you can go back to the menu of chart types and choose another one. The program will quickly generate a new chart based on the same data. Once you have entered the data, the program quickly and easily lets you preview the possible choices before you commit to any one type of chart.

Chart formatting Up to this point you have produced the basic chart, but without titles and legends that make the chart understandable to others. Most graphics programs provide a wide array of formatting options, including labels, titles, legends, colors, line types, fill patterns, and three-dimensional effects. Programs vary widely, however, in the ease of using and changing these options.

One area of business graphics programs that is generally far less flexible than hand-drawn graphics is formatting. Especially with programs that are easy to use, the formatting options can be quite limited. For example, a particular program might print titles in uppercase letters only and in one or two type styles, and labels for the scale might be printed vertically. Obviously, computer-generated business graphics is a very useful application, but the software's limitations often impose compromises in the variety and quality of images.

The chart title is one of the most basic formatting options. You should be able to create titles in several typefaces, or fonts, and with different attributes, such as boldface or underlining. The better programs enable you to position titles anywhere on the chart to help explain unusual entries or trends. This title-positioning feature is called the *floating title.* For example, in an otherwise upward-trending series of data showing profits, your company might show a disastrously low profit for one year. With a movable title, you could position the message "IRS Settlement" at the appropriate point to explain that the Internal Revenue Service assessed your company $2 million in back taxes.

The better programs offer several types of lines for drawing line charts. If you have five types of dashed lines to choose from, for example, you could use one to indicate each of several products, or you could differentiate income and expenditures with different types of lines.

Another useful formatting device is the fill pattern for bar, pie, and area charts. Fill patterns are various combinations of stripes, stipples, and cross-hatching that differentiate enclosed areas in a chart; they are especially useful for stacked bar charts and pie charts. Some graphics programs offer up to six fill patterns.

Many programs offer point markers to use with scatterplot charts. They can be squares, triangles, crosses, or diamonds, for example. You may also be able to create new types of markers by printing one on top of another.

Color can be used effectively to differentiate lines, titles, and areas in a chart. Although the standard background color for most programs is usually black, the better programs offer up to 16 choices of background color. However, when you are working with a business graphics program in color, determining the characteristics of the chart can be a complicated task.

Another problem unique to color graphics is that the characteristics of the program can vary, depending on the type of color monitor you are using. The program should have command settings to optimize the display for each type of monitor, an RGB (red, green, blue) or a composite monitor (a color TV is a composite monitor). If you are using the IBM Monochrome Display simultaneously with a color monitor, the graphics generated by the program will usually be displayed on the color monitor, while the program's commands may be displayed on the monochrome monitor.

In general, an RGB monitor is preferable for graphics because its images are much sharper than those on a television or other composite color monitor. RGB monitors usually feature high resolution—they have a large number of individual dots, or pixels, that make up the images on the screen. The more dots that appear over a given screen area, the sharper the image. Some monitors are bit-addressable or bit-mapped, which means that each of the dots, or pixels, on the screen is represented by one bit, or binary digit, within the computer's memory. The practical effect of bit-mapping is that you can create detailed, sophisticated images on the screen.

When creating graphs in color, you have to make

choices about the background and foreground colors of the chart. Although you will often have a wide choice of background colors, the color choices for lines, titles, and markers may be more limited.

Many programs offer two or three standard combinations of colors for the images, such as red, yellow, and green. The program will automatically change to the next of the three colors each time you add a new element to the chart. The first element will be red, the second yellow, and so on. Although you can vary the order in which the colors are used, you usually can't substitute colors outside the sequence. If you don't like your charts in red, yellow, and green, or whatever other color combinations the program offers, you're out of luck.

One nice feature that some programs offer is the ability to create titles in the same color as an element of the chart, so that a chart's sections and the titles that refer to them are in the same color. This graphic identification makes the individual features of the chart easier to interpret.

You have to be careful with color when you are editing your charts, however. Because programs often cycle through the colors in order, you could end up with some inappropriate color combinations if you edit and rearrange the elements in a chart and then add a new element.

Many programs include a window command, which is a standard feature for creating more than one chart on the same screen or page. With this command, you can split the screen into two or more parts and create a different chart in each space. Multiple charts provide a useful means of comparison. For example, they can show information for the same subject that has changed over time.

Saving and printing charts Once you have installed the proper monitor and printer or plotter and the appropriate interface boards, the processes of saving and printing charts are not complicated. You can save a chart on disk and print or plot as many copies of a chart as you like. Although most programs control saving and printing with menus, some use commands. When choosing a business graphics program, verify that it is compatible with the printer or the plotter you plan to use and that the printing process is simple but flexible.

Most people use dot matrix printers to produce charts, and many use plotters to create presentation-quality material, often in several colors (see Figure 8.3). Although dot matrix printers are definitely quicker than plotters, the quality of the image is usually not as good. If you want high-quality color charts, the plotter is the preferred way to go.

Communicating with Graphics

Now that you know how charts are produced, you might want to know how to select the type of chart that best communicates the information you need to convey. If you want to show comparisons of values at different times, for example, a bar chart is especially useful. You get an immediate sense of relative value by the size of the individual bars. This comparative dimension can be accentuated with three-dimensional bars.

Although the pie chart is similar to the bar chart in that it emphasizes comparative values, it is not useful for showing data that has changed over time. The pie chart is useful, however, for illustrating the relative size of parts of a whole at any one time. A classic use of the pie chart is to show market share for a product among several competitors. The pie gives

Figure 8.3 *Examples of bar charts printed with a dot matrix printer and a plotter (following page).*

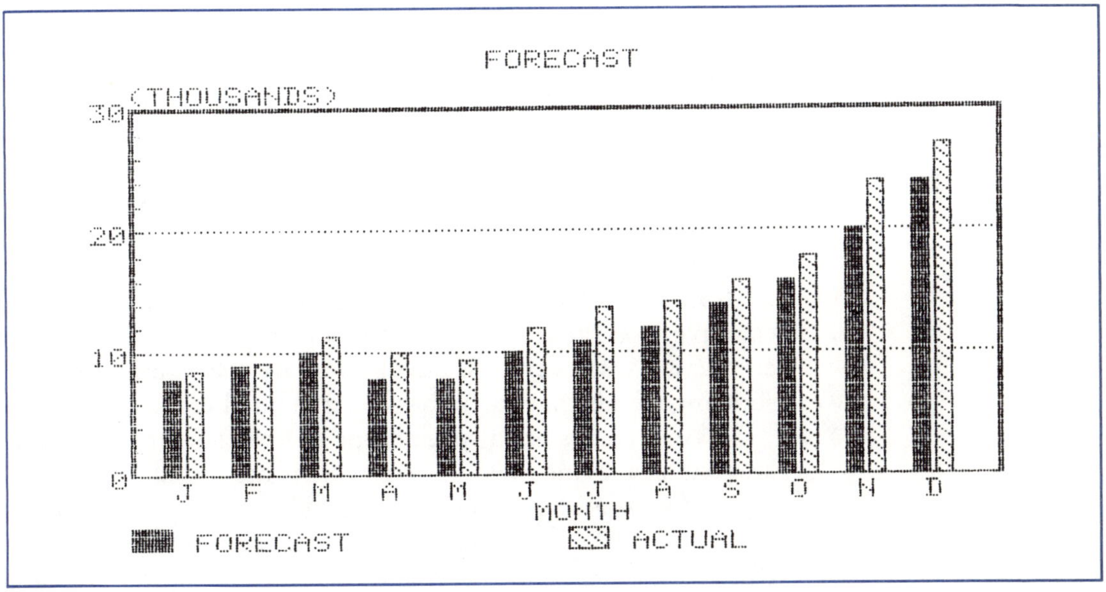

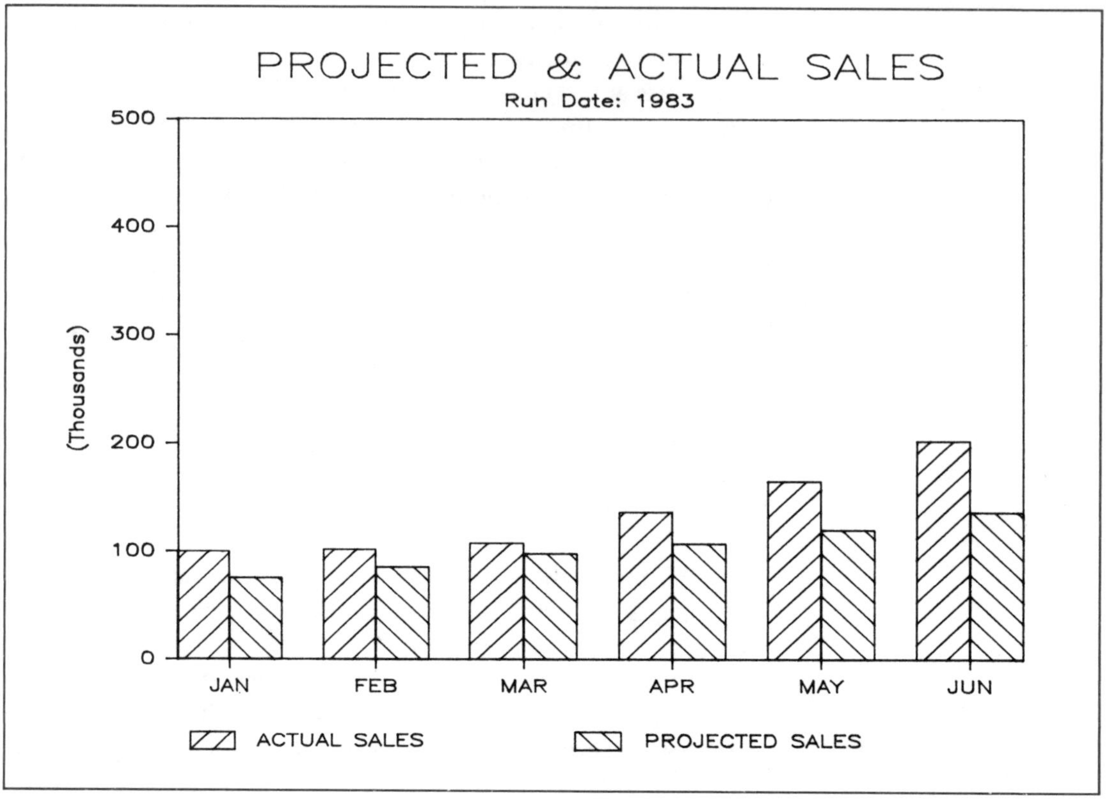

you a "snapshot" of where you stand. By "exploding" a section of the pie and enlarging it, you can give it special emphasis. For example, you might want to explode the section that showed your own company's market share.

Line graphs are usually used to illustrate trends in data over time. They can also be used to compare trends in the same variable for different entities. You could use a line graph to show your company's gross sales for the past ten years, for example, and on the same chart show lines for your major competitors' sales trends. Line graphs are also useful for showing trends that encompass a large number of data points.

Area charts are a special type of line chart that have the area under the line filled in. Area charts are useful for imparting a sense of mass or importance, and stacked area charts can be used like a pie chart to show the relative importance of parts of a whole. Area charts are also very handy for creating profit and loss, or break-even charts, in which the amount of loss or profit is indicated by shading or color, and the break-even point is shown at the point where the profit and loss lines cross.

Time series analysis Many of the best business graphics programs feature time series analysis, which is used to demonstrate and forecast trends in data. A host of functions are included under this title, such as statistical analysis, multiple linear regression, data transformations, data smoothing, and curve fitting.

Most of the programs that include time series analysis do so as part of the overall program and don't place emphasis on these features. *VisiTrend/Plot* (VisiCorp), however, has a whole subprogram devoted to time series analysis that interacts directly with the graphics subprogram. This program is discussed in more detail in the next chapter.

Statistical functions are probably the easiest time series functions to understand and use. For any series of data, the program will calculate the maximum and minimum values, the mean, variance, standard deviation, and coefficient of correlation. These values are displayed in tabular form and can be printed. Most programs offer choices about how you want to display the results, such as how many decimal places a number will have. This type of statistical analysis is useful in determining the significance of series of data and whether or not trends can be inferred from the data.

Some programs, including *VisiTrend/Plot,* can calculate multiple *linear regressions* for a series of numbers using several independent variables. Multiple regression is a useful tool for business forecasting. Regression relates the behavior of a single dependent variable to the behavior of one or more independent variables. In this way, you can predict what the dependent variable is going to do, based on the values and trends of the independent variables.

Suppose you wanted to forecast the direction that the stock market will take. Using the hemlines in women's dresses as an independent variable, you might discover by linear regression analysis that the stock market average correlated closely with the changes in the length of hemlines. When skirts are long, the market goes down. When miniskirts are in fashion, the market goes up. (Believe it or not, there is a strong correlation between the stock market and hemlines.) Multiple linear regression can perform such analysis of trends and can also be used for trend forecasting.

Data smoothing is a technique used commonly in analyzing business trends. Trends in data are frequently skewed by severe fluctuations caused by seasonal factors or unusual occurrences. For instance, data on hospital use shows strong seasonality, with low hospital occupancy in the summer and high occupancy in October and November. This seasonality can distort the underlying trends in the data over time and make it more difficult to analyze.

Data smoothing evens the raggedness by replacing the original data series with a new series formed by computing a moving average. The moving average smooths out the peaks and valleys in the data and generates a curve that is easier to analyze. Although the moving average can be calculated in several ways, the effect is always the same. A similar technique, called *exponential smoothing,* is sometimes used in business graphics programs.

Curve fitting is another feature of some graphics programs that aids in analysis and forecasting. The program will create a curve that best fits a data series. The curve can be a line, an exponential curve, or another type of curve. You can experiment with different types of curves, and the program will produce statistics to show you which is the best fit. Then you can use the curve to generate expected data points for inclusion in a forecast.

Another useful graphics feature is the ability to lead and lag several series of data. The most common use for both of these functions is the linking of data with the time periods for which it is most appropriate. For example, many expenditures in business are made far in advance of the expected result. Research and development (R&D) for a given product is sometimes conducted years before sales revenues for that product are realized. Using the lag function for more meaningful profit analysis, you can shift the R&D expenses forward to the period at which the revenues will come in. The lead function has exactly the opposite purpose.

There are several other mathematical, statistical, and time series analysis features that you might encounter in business graphics programs. Not only do these features vary from program to program, but each program may implement them in different ways. Be sure to inquire about the methodology behind some of these functions, because some are constructed in nonstandard ways that might make their results invalid for serious statistical work.

Graphics Applications

There are many ways to use business graphics produced by the PC and the XT. As already noted, crisp and concise graphics are a great help in analyzing trends in data. The more complex the data and the greater the scope of the task, the more useful the graphics can be. They illuminate trends, highlight problems, and make comparisons easy.

One of the most common uses for this application in business is the charting of spreadsheets. Almost all of the business graphics programs accept *VisiCalc* files in the DIF format, and some programs accept files from other spreadsheets. The interrelationship of these two applications was not lost on software designers who have combined graphics and spreadsheets in numerous integrated programs, such as *1-2-3*, which is examined more closely in Chapter 11.

The best graphics programs are very useful for financial forecasting, one of the toughest business tasks. Programs that have features such as multiple linear regression, curve fitting, and trend line extension can ease the risks involved in budgeting, planning capital expenditures, and investing.

In addition, by converting numbers into images, graphics can make complex data and concepts easily comprehensible. As noted previously, graphics are highly useful for comparing financial and time-period data, but images are equally effective for illustrating scientific, engineering, and other technical information.

Managers frequently use graphics for in-house presentations to co-workers or bosses. Graphics can bring the stalest report to life and make selling your point of view easier. Graphics programs continue to grow in popularity as one of the most interesting and insightful tools available for use with a computer.

CHAPTER NINE

An Introduction to pfs:graph, BGS, BPS, and VisiTrend/Plot

Business graphics programs tend to have the same basic features and implement them in a similar manner. The programs are distinguished for the most part by the variety of options associated with the features, the speed of execution, and price. One notable exception to the similarity in features among graphics programs is *VisiTrend/Plot* (VisiCorp), which produces graphs capable of depicting data for time series analysis.

This chapter introduces four versatile graphics programs. *pfs:graph* (Software Publishing) is a low-cost program that offers the basic graphics functions. Two more sophisticated graphics packages, *Business Graphics System* (Peachtree Software) and *BPS Business Graphics* (Business & Professional Software), offer a full complement of features. And *VisiPlot/Trend,* in addition to providing standard graphics, offers the specialized time series feature.

pfs:graph

pfs:graph is an entry-level program that offers only the basic features of business graphics, but the features are implemented so well that the program is fast and efficient. In fact, the program is so enjoyable to use that you may not miss the sophisticated features it lacks.

As a member of the *pfs:* series of programs, which includes *pfs:file* and *pfs:report* (discussed in Chapter 7), *pfs:graph* can automatically convert data files from other *pfs:* programs into the graph format. Thus, if you use other *pfs:* programs, you may find *pfs:graph* especially efficient for creating basic business graphics.

The program performs automatic data reduction on the files you are reading in, if that is required. For example, suppose that your data file had production costs listed by month, and you wanted to create a graph of annual costs. When reading in the files, *pfs:graph* could consolidate the monthly costs to produce annual totals.

pfs:graph can also read data directly from *VisiCalc* spreadsheet files in the DIF format. *VisiCalc* data can also be reduced by the program.

Documentation As with all *pfs:* programs, the documentation is excellent. Although a quick start course is not included, you really don't need one with a program this basic. The manual is well written and well organized; you can work your way through it in less than an hour and learn all you need to know about the program. The menus and the forms are laid out so well that you could almost run the program without referring to the manual.

Features *pfs:graph* offers three basic charts: bar, line, and pie. You can use color or fill patterns to create area charts out of line charts, however. If the data on your *X*-axis is numeric, the program automatically creates a line chart. If the *X*-axis data is not numeric, the program produces a bar chart. You can override this feature, however, and create any of the three basic chart types. The only types of graphs that can be combined are bar and line. Because pie charts take up the whole screen, you can display only one at a time.

Sets of data in bar charts can be stacked or displayed side by side. If bars are displayed side by side, up to 36 can be used in one chart. Since the program will accept a maximum of four sets of data, you can show comparative results in this format for only up to 9 data points per set. If you stack the bars, however, you can show the program's maximum of 36 data points for each of the four sets of data. With line charts, you can display 144 data points by stacking four separate sets of 36 data points each, one on top of another.

pfs:graph refers to one data set as a graph, and to a composite of one or more sets as a chart; you can have four graphs per chart. Because this terminology is not used in other business graphics programs, it can be confusing.

In addition to accepting numeric and date information as *X* coordinates for a graph, the program also accepts "identifier" *X* coordinates. An identifier is simply a name, such as a region of the country or a division of a company. If *X* coordinates are identifiers, you can have no more than 16 data points per graph in the identifiers to fit on the *X*-axis.

A pie graph must use identifier *X* coordinates, and it can have a maximum of eight slices. *pfs:graph* begins a pie at the largest segment and displays other segments in descending size order. You can't display pie charts with other charts.

pfs:graph can also plot cumulative charts. For example, the topmost bar or line on a chart could be the plot of the total of the *Y* values for each *X* value on all the plots. Or, if you were creating a chart of monthly sales, you might choose to create a cumulative chart. For each month interval across the chart, the total sales are displayed with that month's and all previous months' sales added together. This chart would then display the increase in total sales to date rather than the amount of sales for any specific month.

When it comes to formatting, *pfs:graph* is effective but inflexible. You can't control color, fill patterns, or line markers, other than to specify whether you want them. The program provides all these features automatically. For instance, it produces fill patterns with the darkest at the bottom and alternates successive fill patterns in a visually pleasing format (see Figure 9.1). Some business graphics programs costing much more won't fill bars in this manner.

You can add a main title to a chart, and it will appear centered at the top in capital letters. The *X*- and *Y*-axis labels are displayed in capitals, with the *X*-axis label up to 40 characters long and the *Y*-axis label up to 30 characters long. Pie chart labels appear alongside the chart and include the total value of the pie segments. Because *pfs:graph* can print a sam-

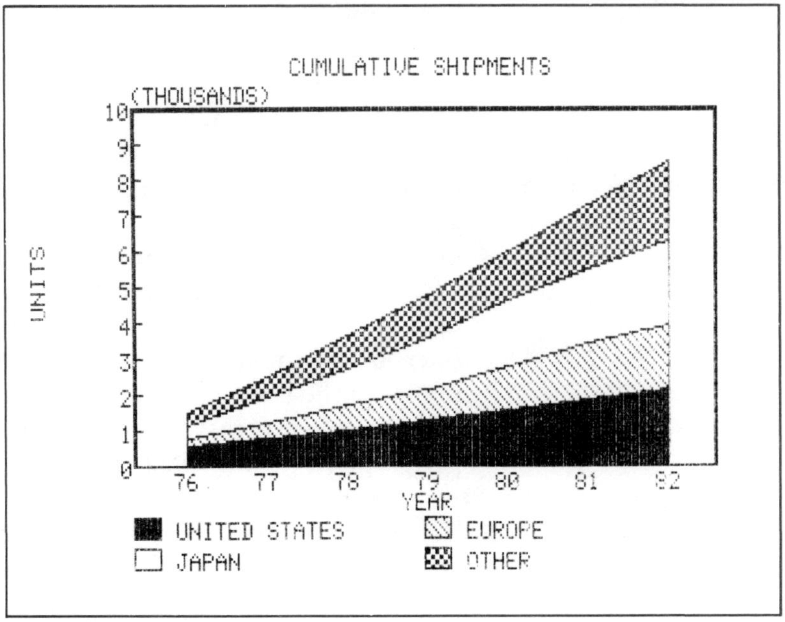

Figure 9.1 *An example of alternating fill pattern in an area graph produced with* pfs:graph.

ple legend at the bottom of a chart, you can label and identify the various symbols used in a chart.

The program uses a menu and an on-screen form to be filled in to create charts. You define the chart's data with the Enter/Edit Data Screen. You can easily return to this screen later and change data entries by typing over them or deleting values and inserting new ones. You can use the PC cursor keys to move around in the form, but you have to make the unconventional switch to <F10> to enter commands, instead of using the <Enter> key.

A Define Chart Menu is used to determine the chart's characteristics, such as type of chart, titles, and legends. Most formatting is done by answering yes/no questions. The whole process of defining the chart is quick and easy.

pfs:graph supports the most popular printers and plotters, including the IBM and Epson dot matrix printers, and several Hewlett-Packard and Houston Instruments plotters. The installation program for printers and plotters is easy to use. *pfs:graph* requires only one disk drive and 128K of RAM.

If your business graphics needs are simple, or if you want a program that will help you learn the basics of creating usable business graphics, *pfs:graph* is an excellent choice.

Business Graphics System

Although *BGS* is limited in the amounts of data it can use to create different types of charts, and it has an awkward method of labeling charts and graphs, its features make it one of the leading business graphics programs. Among its more desirable features are three-dimensional bar charts and several special types of charts, such as a critical ratio graph not found in most other such programs.

Documentation Like the program itself, the documentation for *BGS* is both good and bad. It includes an installation and configuration manual, a reference card, a card on converting spreadsheet files to *BGS* files, and the program manual. The program manual includes a Quick Start section, a tutorial, a section called "Using BGS," as well as a glossary and an index. Although the manual is well written and easy to understand, its poor organization forces you to flip between the front and the back to find information. The Quick Start section is too brief to teach much, and the index is not comprehensive. For instance, the index omits an entry for *linear regression* or *regression,* even though the program can perform this operation.

Features When it comes to the number of charts offered, *BGS* is one of the best business graphics programs. It creates line, bar, and area charts with some interesting variations. For example, bar charts can be three-dimensional with perspective from side to side or top to bottom (see Figure 9.2). You can also create conventional bar graphs with bars displayed horizontally and each bar representing a part of a total amount. Also possible is a double-sided bar graph that shows two charts back to back to compare two sets of data. These double-sided charts are rarely found in other business graphics programs.

Another seldom-encountered chart available in *BGS* is a critical ratio graph, which uses up to three pairs of horizontal bars to show key financial ratios, such as debt to equity. The chart can show data for two time periods, with the numerical values of the ratios displayed on the right side.

BGS also provides a specialized bar chart called a histogram, which shows the frequency of an occurrence within specified ranges. For example, it can show the number of em-

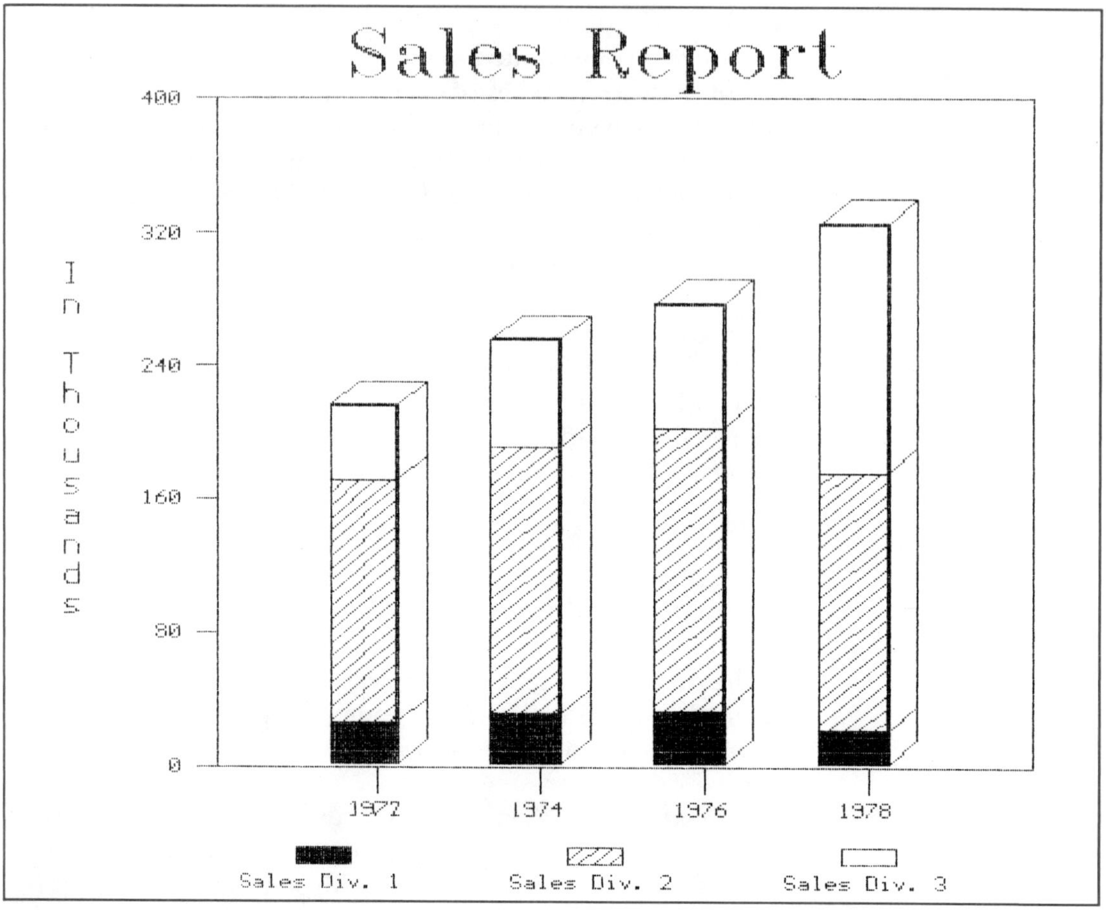

Figure 9.2 *A three-dimensional bar chart produced with* Business Graphics System (BGS).

ployees in a company within certain age ranges. *BGS* represents the frequency with a vertical bar, and each bar is the width of a range.

The program can also create scatterpoint charts and pie charts that have up to 12 slices per pie. One slice of a pie chart can be "exploded" for emphasis (see Figure 9.3).

BGS is somewhat awkward in labeling charts, however. It uses what it calls a "word graph" for adding labels to existing *BGS* charts and creating all-text transparencies. But you can't position discretionary, or "floating," labels in a chart while you are creating it. To do that, you have to go back to the main menu and create a word graph that positions the labels where you want them.

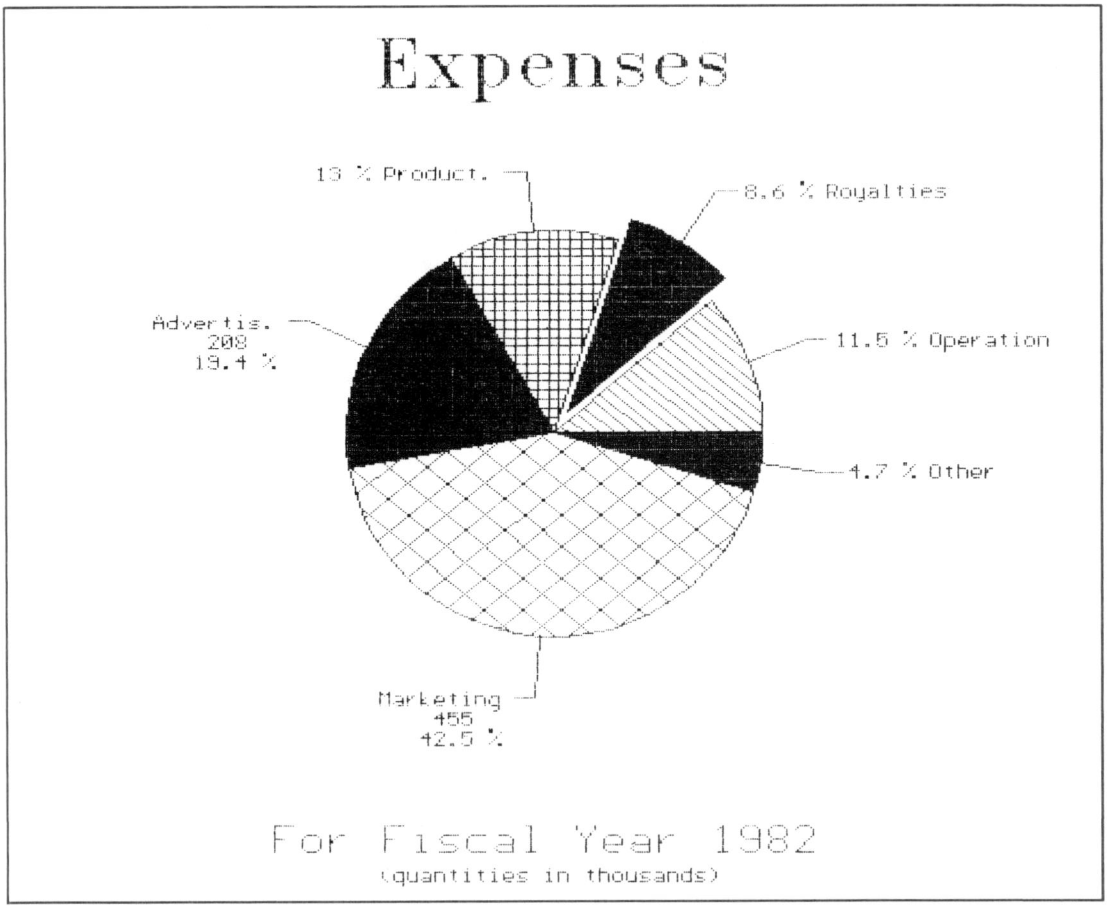

Figure 9.3 *An exploded pie chart produced with* BGS.

Despite its awkwardness in labeling, *BGS* has other good formatting features. You can create graphs with up to nine types of fill patterns and six line styles. And you can choose from seven fonts for the main title. All the other labels on the graph are in small type. Some of the type styles, notably Gothic and Script, are not particularly useful for business charts. You can also make the characters in titles and labels slant backward or forward for emphasis, but the results may be strange.

If you are using the IBM Color/Graphics Adapter and a color monitor, you can choose either of two sets of four colors to display data. All eight possible colors can be used for titles, axes, and point markers.

BGS is limited in the number of data points and sets of data it can chart. The greatest number of points available with a bar chart is 32 if you have one or two sets of data to chart. If there are three or more data sets (up to a maximum of five), you can chart up to 12 data points per set. You can stack a maximum of five bar or line charts.

BGS supports a single time series analysis function. As an automatic part of the scatterpoint chart, *BGS* will plot a linear regression line and print out the *Y* intercept, the slope of the line, and the coefficient of correlation. Some other business graphics programs, notably *VisiTrend/Plot* and *BPS,* offer more time series analysis functions.

The program will accept data files from at least three spreadsheet programs: *PeachCalc* (part of *PeachText 5000*), *SuperCalc,* and *VisiCalc.* The program has a special data conversion utility that changes spreadsheet files into a format that can be graphed.

To create a chart with *BGS,* you use a fill-in-the-blanks method similar to some data base management programs. After you choose to create a new chart through the program's main menu, *BGS* presents you with a Label Form on which you fill in data fields that specify the characteristics of your chart (see Figure 9.4). Then the program presents you with a Data Form on which to enter the actual numbers for the sets of data selected.

Although the Data Form is easy to use, the Label Form is another story. You have to fill in a lot of information, and the program doesn't provide much help as you enter codes. For novices unfamiliar with the codes, filling in a Label Form is time consuming, but once you become familiar with the codes, the process goes rather quickly. You use the PC cursor keys to move the cursor within the forms as you edit or complete them.

BGS supports three popular dot matrix printers and eight plotters, and you can use the IBM Monochrome Display as a command monitor if you like.

Although Peachtree has a reputation for good customer support, the only provision for technical support is a 90-day limited warranty for the replacement of defective disks.

With the exception of its limitations in labeling and capacity, *BGS* compares favorably with most business graphics programs available for the PC and the XT.

Title of Chart: ______________________________ Color of Title: ________
Font of Title: _____ Char Height: _____ Char Width: _____ Char Slant: _____
Title of Vertical Axis: ____________________

(L)ine, (B)ar or (A)rea Chart: _____ (S)tacked or (C)omparison: _____
Horizontal Perspective: _____ Vertical Perspective: _____

Number of Stacked/Comparison Groups (1–5): _____

	Group Label	Color	Fill Pattern	Line Marker
(1):	____________________	________	__	__
(2):	____________________	________	__	__
(3):	____________________	________	__	__
(4):	____________________	________	__	__
(5):	____________________	________	__	__

Number of Data Points Per Group (1–12): _____
X-axis Labels (V)ertical, (H)orizontal or (A)ngled: _____
Labels of Each Data Point:
(1): _____ (2): _____ (3): _____ (4): _____ (5): _____ (6): _____
(7): _____ (8): _____ (9): _____ (10): _____ (11): _____ (12): _____
Frame Chart (Y/N)?: _____ Type of Minor Tics (0–3): _____
Vertical Axis Scaling Override: Ymin: ____________ Ymax: ____________

Figure 9.4 *The Label Form provided by* BGS *for specifying the characteristics of a chart.*

BPS Business Graphics

BPS has more features than most other business graphics programs. The program requires a good deal of study, however, because it is command-driven and has a total of 101 system commands to learn.

Documentation The *BPS* documentation is good. The manual is typeset, well illustrated, and bound in a three-ring binder. Although the manual is voluminous, given the complexity of the program, you will appreciate all the information. An excellent section on general business graphics provides helpful hints on using charts appropriately for different jobs. Also included are a glossary and a detailed index. A Pocket Reference Card and a large schematic of the program's menus serve as quick references to the program's features.

Of the manual's seven chapters, one is a primer on business graphics, another provides a tutorial on working with the program, and a third demonstrates advanced graphing techniques. Another chapter provides helpful examples and applications for each of the major chart types. You learn not only how to use the program better, but also how to apply business graphics to real jobs. The concluding chapters focus on printing and on specialized features of the program.

Features *BPS* can create vertical and horizontal bar charts, line charts, area charts, and pie charts. The program does not offer some of the more exotic chart types, such as critical ratio or high-low-close. The basic charts, however, offer latitude for customization, and you can combine line charts with both bar and area charts.

BPS can accommodate a large amount of data in a single chart. You can have up to 4000 data entries for one set of data. With bar charts, you can chart up to five data sets at one time, with bars stacked five high or side by side. For bar, area, and pie charts, seven fill patterns are available, including solid and unfilled. For line charts, five kinds of dashed lines and eight types of point markers can be used. Pie charts can be drawn without fill patterns, and you can create pies that have missing slices to emphasize the remainder.

You can use colors with fill patterns, lines, and point markers. *BPS* offers 16 background colors and two sets of three colors each for fill patterns, lines, and axes. The default color set is green, red, and yellow, but you can choose an alternate set of cyan, magenta, and white. Although the program automatically cycles through the color sets, you can also assign a color to any item. You can use a Set command to choose line type, point marker, or fill pattern for specific charts.

BPS is especially flexible in applying titles and labels. You can create labels for the *X* and *Y* axes in both horizontal and vertical format. You can place vertical or horizontal floating titles anywhere within the axes of a chart and label slices of a pie chart (see Figure 9.5). You position floating titles with the cursor keys. Floating titles can also be combined with other characters, such as dashed lines or point markers, to form legends. When you create floating titles in color, they are the same color as the last chart element formed.

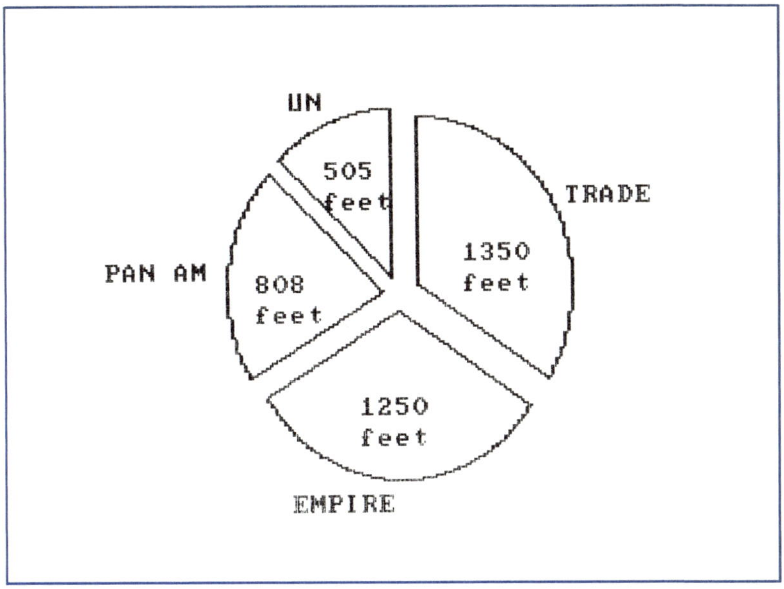

Figure 9.5 *An example of the flexibility of labeling with* BPS Business Graphics. *Labels can be added at any point inside or outside the sections of a chart.*

To further customize a chart, you can add horizontal or vertical grid lines, or both (similar to graph paper). Rather than using labels on the axes, you can draw charts with only numbers on both axes. Although *BPS* doesn't offer a choice of type styles for titles, it employs a type style in capital letters that is suitable for business purposes.

BPS can transform data with mathematical operations, such as addition, subtraction, multiplication, and division. You can use these functions to change the *Y* values in a chart and create new relationships. You might use multiplication, for example, to convert dollars to another currency and create a chart with the *Y*-axis in francs or marks.

Related to the math functions are the *BPS* time series analysis functions. You can use the Smooth Moving Average function to smooth out the irregularities in a data series and portray an accurate picture of trends. *BPS* also supports curve fitting, with several types of curves available.

To use these advanced features, you have to know the *BPS* command structure. The program isn't easy to learn, however, because it provides a minimal amount of prompts and other on-screen help. Help screens are available for the major commands only. Although the *BPS* command syntax is somewhat difficult to learn, once you know it you can work efficiently without being slowed down by layers of menus and prompts.

One excellent feature of *BPS* is the ability to automate the creation of charts and graphs with subprograms called Take files. You can create a Take file, which is simply a string of *BPS* commands, save it, and use it again to recreate any chart used routinely. Other, more creative uses for Take files are, of course, possible, such as using several Take files to create a series of charts automatically while making a business presentation. The Take files will draw charts in sequence on the screen, and you can add text messages if you want.

BPS is also excellent in accepting data from other programs. An Interchange function is provided for converting data from any program that can produce a printed report. The Interchange command enables you to access and create graphs for *Multiplan* files, as well as for files produced by *VisiCalc, SuperCalc, dBASE II, WordStar,* and many other programs.

BPS can print charts on dot matrix printers, letter quality printers, and plotters. The program supports at least 25 of these devices, including several models of each.

BPS requires 128K of memory (for DOS 2.00), two floppy disk drives, and the IBM Color/Graphics Adapter to show graphics.

Although *BPS* isn't simple to learn, it is one of the most full-featured, powerful business graphics programs available for the PC and the XT.

VisiTrend/Plot

Although most advanced business graphics programs have several time series analysis features, *VisiTrend/Plot* has a complete subprogram devoted to these operations. In fact, the time series analysis features are its main strength as a graphics program. *VisiTrend/Plot* has good support and excellent documentation, but other factors, such as a limited number of fill patterns and line types, limited labeling capability, and the lack of color in charts, make it an otherwise average graphics package.

Documentation VisiCorp has a reputation for strong customer support and some of the best documentation in the business. The documentation for *VisiTrend/Plot* is no exception. It includes a manual, a Pocket Reference Card, and a User Support Plan. All the material is written specifically for the IBM PC and XT version of the program.

The manual includes tutorial and reference sections. Included with the program is an "example diskette" for use with the tutorial. The manual's table of contents and index are thorough. Detailed instructions for using the program are included, with key-by-key guides for all *VisiTrend/Plot*'s features. Improving this documentation would be difficult.

Features Like most standard graphics programs, *VisiTrend/Plot* offers bar, line, area, and pie charts. Also provided are high-low-close charts for tracking stock prices and scatterpoint plots. With the exception of the pie chart, most charts can be combined to produce special comparisons and customized charts.

Although *VisiTrend/Plot* offers the most commonly used charts, it has some limitations. The program does not present charts in color but in shades of gray. And titles can be produced in only one font, unlike some of the more sophisticated programs that offer several fonts and sizes.

Formatting options with this program are also limited. There are only three choices for fill patterns on bar and area charts, two of which are solid and outline. Only one type of line can be drawn, but six types of point markers are available to differentiate lines. The program can display a legend with up to six entries. You can add horizontal and vertical grid lines to a chart, and display charts with or without *X*- or *Y*-axis labels.

The program is somewhat better when it comes to titles. You can create a main title at the top of a chart, either centered or left justified, in normal, inverse, or boldface characters. You can also enter up to three subtitles at the bottom of a chart. The title for the *Y*-axis is always vertical. *VisiTrend/Plot* also supports floating titles in normal, inverse, or boldface type.

If you don't like the appearance of the axes on a chart, you can override the program's automatic control of the scale and the range. *VisiTrend/Plot* also offers a Window feature that lets you create two charts on the same page, and a Text function that enables you to create charts with all text or to

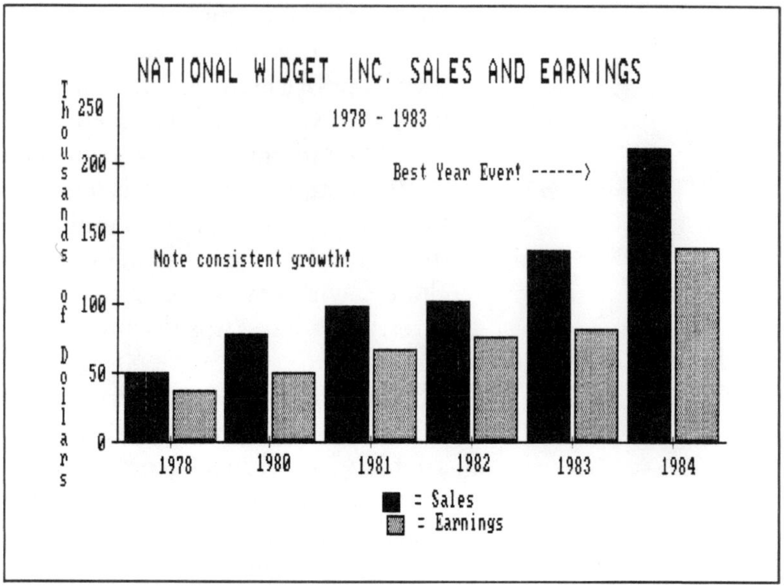

Figure 9.6 *An example of the labeling flexibility provided by* VisiPlot/Trend.

place text anywhere on a chart (see Figure 9.6).

If *VisiTrend/Plot* were evaluated on the basis of its graphics capabilities alone, it would be an average program at best. But its Trend module for time series analysis sets the program apart from other business graphics packages.

The program has three basic time series menu options: Analyze, which includes multiple linear regression, trend line forecasting, and common statistics such as variance and standard deviation; Function, which includes moving average, leading and lagging series, and exponential smoothing; and Xform, which transforms existing data series into new series through mathematical and logical operations.

For any given set of data, *VisiTrend/Plot* generates a full complement of statistical measures, including count, maximum, minimum, mean, variance, and standard deviation. Whereas these functions are useful for analyzing what has already happened, the Multiple Linear Regression function is a tool for predicting what is going to happen. Regression can be used to relate the behavior of a dependent variable to the behavior of up to five independent variables. For example, you might want to relate the behavior of the pork bellies futures market to the weather or the corn harvest in the Midwest.

With *VisiTrend/Plot,* you could run a multiple linear regression for historical data on weather, corn harvests, and the pork bellies market to determine if the behavior of the dependent variable—the market—is linearly linked to the behavior of the independent variables—the weather and corn harvest.

You can use the same regression function to do trend forecasting. The program will fit a straight line for the dependent variable in a historical data series and will extend the straight line for a specified number of periods. You can get a rough idea of what to expect for the dependent variable in the years or the months ahead if there are no major changes in the behavior of the independent variables.

The scope and the depth of *VisiTrend/Plot*'s time series analysis features are outstanding, and combined with the business graphics capabilities, they make a powerful analytic and forecasting tool. The Trend module is a straightforward, menu-driven component that novices should find easy to learn. On-screen prompts and messages help you through each step of the program.

VisiTrend/Plot requires a system that has at least 192K of RAM and an IBM Color/Graphics Adapter. Any graphics-capable monitor will work, including a color monitor, but the program won't display in color. VisiCorp offers a 90-day limited warranty, a customer service hot line, and credit toward purchasing future enhanced versions of the program.

Although business graphics per se are not *VisiTrend/Plot*'s forte, if you need graphics bundled with powerful time series analysis functions, *VisiTrend/Plot* is definitely a program to consider.

CHAPTER TEN

Integrated Programs

What most people mean when they call a program "integrated" is that the software has several applications programs on the same disk and that data can be moved directly from one application to another. A good example of such an integrated program is *1-2-3* (Lotus Development Corporation), which offers an electronic spreadsheet, a data base manager, and graphics all in one package.

1-2-3 was the first program to raise the consciousness of microcomputer users about program integration. A number of other programs for the PC and the XT are also integrated, but in ways quite different from *1-2-3*. Essentially, integrated software falls into three major divisions: software families, multi-application programs, and operating environments.

Families of programs, such as the VisiSeries from VisiCorp, the "Star" products from MicroPro, and the *pfs:* group from Software Publishing constitute the simplest form of integration. Each of these families features a group of separate applications programs. In some, each program is a major application; in others, a dominant program in the family is surrounded by a number of support programs. For example, in the VisiSeries, the *VisiCalc* spreadsheet is often the dominant application, and such programs as *VisiTrend/Plot* provide support for it. Although each program in an integrated family is self-contained, and generally on a separate disk, they all can use the same data files.

This can be an important advantage when information must be shared among several applications. A customer list, for example, might be used for form letters and mailing labels (word processing), invoices (accounting or spreadsheet), and inventory maintenance (data base mangement).

The next level of program integration is the multiapplication program. At this level, several business applications programs are contained on one or more disks, and you can work with the same data in different ways, usually without shutting down one application and loading another from a separate disk. Although *1-2-3* is a typical multiapplication program, *MBA* (Context Management) was the first such program for the PC. Many others are now available from various manufacturers.

Multiapplication programs generally have a dominant application, like some software families. *1-2-3,* for example, is based on a very large and powerful spreadsheet. In fact, many people buy *1-2-3* for the spreadsheet alone and use the other applications minimally at first. Many multiapplication programs feature a spreadsheet as the cornerstone of the package, most often combining a graphics component with it. Other multiapplication programs have a data base manager as the hub application, such as *Open Access* (SPI).

There is no typical number of applications for a multiapplication program. For instance, *Open Access* provides data base management, spreadsheet, graphics, word processing, communications, and time management components. Some programs, such as *SuperCalc3,* have only two applications: an electronic spreadsheet and graphics.

The most sophisticated level of software integration for the PC and the XT is the operating environment. In terms of integration, an operating environment can support multiple active applications. For example, an operating environment might enable you to access and run several programs at once. Although there is no uniformity in the structure of these programs, they generally have similar features.

Some operating environments enable you to move from

DESQ

Open New Window	O
Switch Windows	S
Rearrange Windows	R
Close Window	C
File & Print	F
Learn	=
Mark & Transfer	M
View	V
Help	?
Install & Setup	I
Quit DESQ	Q
DESQ Scripts	+

Figure 10.1 *The main menu of* DesQ, *an operating environment designed to work with a variety of programs.*

one application to another quickly. Most such programs provide windowing capability, so that you can view several files simultaneously. To provide these sophisticated features, an operating environment requires a system that has a lot of memory, a large storage capacity, and a powerful CPU. The PC, and especially the XT, are ideal for this type of integrated software.

Operating environments are now rapidly appearing on the microcomputer market. One of the first was *Visi On* from VisiCorp. Quarterdeck Office Systems offers an operating environment called *DesQ*, and Microsoft has an environment called *Windows*. Others are sure to follow. (Figure 10.1 shows the *DesQ* main menu.)

Software Families

Software families are the least elegant form of integration, but their integrated approach to personal computing is useful, especially for the first-time buyer or the person who doesn't need the power of an operating environment or a multiapplication program.

Within product families, a common file structure is an important integration feature that enables you to exchange data among programs. The VisiSeries of programs uses a structure called Data Interchange Format (DIF). If you are using one of the VisiSeries programs and want to transfer files to another in the group, you save your data in the DIF format.

Sometimes programs that are not in the same product family can also share data. Because *VisiCalc* has been so popular, many other software producers have designed their programs to accept the DIF format. Thus, nearly all the business graphics programs accept files from a *VisiCalc* spreadsheet, and some graphics programs accept other spreadsheet files. This saves the person using the graphics program from having to reenter data produced by a spreadsheet.

File compatibility is no small matter for the average business. Assume for a moment that you have bought a data base management program and have taken weeks to convert all your paper files into electronic data. If you purchased a word processing program that had a file structure incompatible with the data manager's, the word processor wouldn't be able to share data with the data base program; at times you would have to retype information that the data base manager had already produced.

Product families also feature a wide range of applications programs designed to complement one another. A typical range of programs includes spreadsheet, data base management, graphics, and word processing. In some families, supporting programs are grouped around one or more major applications. For example, you might find a spelling checker, a mailing list manager, and a thesaurus supporting a word processing program, as in *PeachText 5000* (Peachtree Software), a program family that is sold as a single unit, rather than as individual programs.

Other software families provide several major components and several support components, such as MicroPro's *WordStar Professional*, which offers *WordStar* word processing as the major component, and *CorrectStar, MailMerge*, and *StarIndex* as support programs. The advantage of this modular software is that a full range of programs is available, even though you may want to start with only one or two. You can add programs as you need them and be assured of compatibility.

BOONE CORPORATION

Welcome to Boone Corporation. What task
do you want to accomplish?

1. Write a letter
2. Add names to the customer file
3. Prepare mailing labels
4. Help! I need explanation of the options!

^J for more info

Choice: ___

Tree = A:Sales   Menu = MAINMENU

Figure 10.2 *A sample menu produced with* StarBurst, *the applications manager for the MicroPro family of programs.*

An often overlooked feature of integration common to product families is similar command and menu structures, which is a great timesaver for anyone thinking about buying a second program. After learning one program's structure and idiosyncrasies, you can add another application without having to learn a new set of procedures.

Some software families feature a program that functions as a kind of traffic manager for the other applications. MicroPro, for example, offers *StarBurst,* which you use to create menus that simplify switching among various applications in the family of programs (see Figure 10.2). *StarBurst,* in effect, functions as a rudimentary operating environment.

Despite their separate module structure, software families have many appealing features. They are usually inexpensive, easy to use, and cover a broad range of important business functions. They sometimes lack the degree of integration available in multiapplication programs, however.

Multiapplication Programs

It was only a matter of time before software designers took the logical step of combining two or more applications on the same disk. As good as individual applications programs may be, people don't necessarily work on just one facet of a job at a time and may be inconvenienced by the need to switch between applications. Anyone who is doing financial analysis for a report, for example, will want to use a spreadsheet and produce graphs of the results. If that same person needs to sort or retrieve the data that goes into the spreadsheet, a data base manager may also be needed. The process of switching between programs on separate disks can be both time-consuming and irritating.

Articles reviewing multiapplication programs praise them for giving people the opportunity to work more creatively. But in fact, the opposite is true. These programs enable people to work as they used to, before personal computing forced them to deal with different functions in a linear manner. There is a trade-off involved in using a multiapplication program, however. Because the size of the combined modules is often limited to a specified amount of memory (typically 256K) or disk capacity (such as 320K), the individual modules are often not as comprehensive as standalone packages devoted to the same function.

A typical multiapplication program has two or more applications modules on the same disk, and the modules are usually directly interactive—that is, you can switch from one to another without having to close a file or exit from the currently active module. Some of these programs also have more than one disk in the package, however. *1-2-3,* for example, has a separate disk that produces graphics. Even with a multiapplication program, you might have to contend with some disk swapping.

One of three possible applications is dominant in some multiapplication programs: spreadsheet, data base management, or word processing. Other multiapplication packages attempt to balance the applications evenly, such as *Framework* (Ashton-Tate), which combines data management, word and idea processing, spreadsheet, and graphics.

The spreadsheet is most commonly used as the central application in multiapplication programs because of its almost universal popularity among managers. In addition, the column-and-row format of a spreadsheet lends itself to the record-and-field structure of a data base manager. In fact, because powerful formatting commands are inherent in most spreadsheets, such as inserting and deleting columns, and moving whole ranges of cells, the data base can be much more flexible than many stand-alone data base management programs. As *1-2-3* demonstrates, spreadsheet and data base functions can be combined in one application.

One limiting factor in the data base module of some multiapplication programs, however, is the amount of data that can be manipulated and recorded, which is often restricted by the size of the spreadsheet itself. Obviously, if the spreadsheet has 2048 rows and 256 columns, as *1-2-3* does, your maximum file size is 2048 records having 256 fields each. If you need a large, full-featured data base manager, you probably shouldn't use a multiapplication program. In general, the forte of these programs is the convenience of switching among applications.

The spreadsheet modules of some of these programs don't suffer the same limitations found in the data base functions. *1-2-3* has a spreadsheet second to none, including the stand-alone variety. It is large, exceedingly fast, and has just about every feature available today. The speed of *1-2-3* is probably its most striking feature. A close competitor is *MBA,* which includes word processing and communications applications as well as spreadsheet, graphics, and data base management capabilities. Compared to *1-2-3, MBA* is slow, but for many people, *MBA*'s extra applications are worth the wait. Lotus Development's *Symphony* combines the impressive *1-2-3* spreadsheet with telecommunications and word processing. This program requires a large amount of memory, however, and is more difficult to learn than either *1-2-3* or *MBA.*

The graphics modules of most multiapplication programs can produce the standard types of charts and can utilize color. Formatting features, such as titles, labels, and fill patterns, are available, as well as automatic scaling. As with data base management, the real value of the graphics application in these programs is the convenience of having it directly accessible from other applications.

Word processing, when it is not the central application, tends to suffer most from the compromises involved in integration. Integrated programs typically lack the outstanding special features that characterize many stand-alone word processors. Although *MBA* has an adequate word processing module, if you are accustomed to using one of the better stand-alone programs, you may not be impressed with *MBA*'s word processing capabilities.

Operating Environments

Although they are not perfect, operating environments are the easiest, fastest, and most useful way to integrate several applications on a personal computer. The term *operating environment* might seem obscure or even pretentious until you consider it carefully. An operating environment is simply an extension of the familiar operating system that takes care of the housekeeping chores for the computer. In this case, however, the portion of the operating system that enables you to run programs is enhanced dramatically to create an "environment" that includes such features as windows, multiple applications, icons, and mouse controllers to help you run different applications during the course of your work.

Some of the operating environments are clearly superior to others in facilitating this critical switch from stand-alone to operating environment programs. The ideal operating environment is one that enables you to use off-the-shelf programs as if they were parts of integrated packages. Applications software must be rewritten to fit into some of these new environments.

The software for an operating environment consists of the management software (the environment itself) and several applications that run under it. *Visi On* (VisiCorp), for example, one of the first operating environments, offers *Visi On* (operating environment), *Visi On Calc* (spreadsheet), *Visi On Word* (word processing), and *Visi On Graph* (business graphics). In this case, VisiCorp has developed all the applications software itself, although the firm encourages other software designers to create new applications programs.

Quarterdeck Office Systems has taken a different approach with *DesQ,* which is designed to run off-the-shelf MS-DOS or PC-DOS programs from other manufacturers without modifications. In this way, *DesQ* takes advantage of the large range of popular software for the PC, the XT, and compatible machines. *Windows,* Microsoft's operating environment, is also designed to work with a variety of PC-DOS and MS-DOS programs, but the programs must be specially adapted to run with *Windows.*

Although most operating environments are menu-driven, some use icons, or symbols, instead of the usual number or letter commands found in most menus. A trash can could represent the delete command, or a file folder could stand for "file." Although most operating environments for the PC still use English commands in the menus, newer generations of software are likely to incorporate more icons and other graphics into their on-screen personalities.

Some operating environments support the use of a mouse, a palm-sized electronic device that controls the movement of a pointer on the monitor. As you slide the mouse over a flat surface, such as the desktop, or over a special pad, the pointer moves around the screen. In this way you can move the cursor, without using the cursor keys, immediately to any point on the screen. To select a command, you move the pointer to the command on the menu, and press a button on the mouse. Because you don't have to remember keystroke sequences with a mouse, operating a program with one is very fast.

Most operating environments that incorporate the use of a mouse also let you enter commands from the keyboard, for convenience. With applications such as word processing, it can be inconvenient to switch between the mouse and the keyboard to enter and edit text and run the program.

Although windows have been a common feature in word processing and spreadsheet programs for some time, in operating environments they are especially useful. You can view a word processing file in one window, a spreadsheet in another, and graphics in another. The windows can be of different sizes, according to the needs of the application. You can also transfer data from one window to another.

Generally, one application runs at a time, and the files displayed in other windows wait until you activate them. You designate one window as the "active" window with the pointer, and you can switch between active windows as needed. Newer versions of operating environments are expected to have *multitasking,* so that more than one application can be active at a time. Soon you will be able to perform some reformatting or printing in a word processing program while you use the electronic spreadsheet.

Although all operating environments use windows, they don't all implement them the same way. *Visi On* uses overlapping windows: portions of windows are covered by other windows, like papers stacked on a desktop. *Windows* uses a process called "tiling" to display its windows; instead of overlapping, they are displayed edge to edge. When new windows are added, the existing windows automatically decrease in size to accommodate the newcomer. Of course, with either type of windowing method, you can change both the size and the position of each individual window using commands or a mouse.

Each window in an operating environment displays its own menus, titles, and prompts. In each window, *Visi On* displays a title line at the top, a prompt line at the bottom, an application menu line, and a menu line for the *Visi On* program. *Windows* has a similar arrangement but uses icons in its window display. *Windows* also has scroll bars that enable you to move information into view. Scrolling is performed by placing the pointer on the scroll bar to direct the program to scroll vertically or horizontally. All operating environments support scrolling within windows, although they don't all use the scroll bar method.

Windows offers one feature that many other operating environments don't offer: bit-mapped graphics. As noted in Chapter 8, bit-mapped or bit-addressable graphics facilitate sharp graphic images. Another integrated operating environment that offers bit-mapped graphics is *Data Base Manager II–The Integrator* (Alpha Software). This environment takes a different approach to integration by including a fully integrated data base management module with the package, and then allowing you to add on a word processing and spreadsheet program of your choice. You can choose from most of the popular programs for the PC and the XT, such as *VisiCalc, 1-2-3, WordStar,* or *Volkswriter Executive* (Lifetree Software). Spreadsheets that have graphics capabilities, such as *1-2-3* and *SuperCalc3,* can take advantage of the superior display characteristics of *Data Base Manager II.*

Of all the operating environments for the PC and the XT, *DesQ* and *Windows* have taken what probably will prove to be the most popular approach to integration. They provide the standard features of an operating environment and enable you to use a variety of software. You don't have to wait for new applications to be written for a specific operating environment. You can combine several of the best programs on the market and structure a system that suits your needs. Consider an operating environment that includes *1-2-3* as the spreadsheet, *Word* as the word processor, and *R:base 4000* as the data base management system. That's horsepower! And all in an easy-to-use, integrated system.

Windows has another feature that is likely to make it popular with software designers. Programs written to operate with *Windows* can run on any computer that *Windows* runs on. If a software designer writes a program that works with *Windows,* he or she doesn't have to worry about the hardware characteristics of different computers. Software that operates with the PC will also work with the TI Professional, the Compaq, the Columbia, and the Eagle. More than 20 computers currently support *Windows.* If you use *Windows,* you have extensive portability for your software among many different machines. You can use the same software and data files for home and business interchangeably.

Operating environments involve some special hardware considerations. *Visi On* requires a PC that has 512K of RAM and a hard disk, or an XT that has 512K. *DesQ* requires a PC that has 512K of RAM and a 5-megabyte hard disk, or an XT that has 512K of RAM. *Windows* requires only 192K of RAM and two floppy disk drives. A hard disk is recommended for *Windows,* however, to enable you to handle operations involving lots of data.

Although operating environments are exciting, there is still a place for software that is part of a product family, and certainly for the multiapplication programs. All three offer valuable integration features.

The applications for integrated programs are not any different from applications for stand-alone programs. The main advantages of integration are convenience, speed, and ease of use. Integrated programs can help you tackle huge, complicated tasks in an organized manner. The following chapter introduces three of the most popular integrated software packages for the PC.

CHAPTER ELEVEN

An Introduction to 1-2-3, PeachText 5000, and Visi On

An early stumbling block for microcomputer users was the inability of different programs to share data. A word processing program, for example, couldn't directly accept figures produced by a spreadsheet program—you had to retype them. A data base manager could generate information ideal for incorporation in a spreadsheet, but because the programs had different methods of reading and formatting data, they couldn't share information. Microcomputer users were left with the prospect of painstakingly reentering the output from one program as input for another.

The primary motivation behind software integration appears to be convenience to the user. People naturally want one program that can handle all their computing needs without their having to worry about file compatibility. But microcomputer users found themselves switching from program to program and juggling disks in and out of the computer as they worked. This problem led software designers to develop integrated programs that offer several applications that are easily accessible by pressing one or two keys.

One of the most successful multiapplication programs to date is *1-2-3,* which consists of three applications that link spreadsheet, data base, and graphics functions. The success of this integrated package has stimulated software developers to develop more integrated products with additional applications. Another product discussed in this chapter, *PeachText 5000,* is really a family of programs sold in one package. It combines word processing, an electronic thesaurus, a spelling checker, a list manager, and an electronic spreadsheet. The final product discussed here is *Visi On,* the operating environment created by VisiCorp.

1-2-3

1-2-3 is an excellent and fast program that provides three important business applications, including a spreadsheet that is second to none. It's a well-integrated package, with the graphics and data management functions directly accessible from the spreadsheet. Just as *VisiCalc* made the Apple II popular, *1-2-3* has sold a tremendous number of IBM PCs and XTs.

The dominant application of *1-2-3* is the spreadsheet. *1-2-3* provides advanced spreadsheet features surpassing those of *VisiCalc* and *Multiplan,* and it incorporates the ability to use information recorded in the spreadsheet cells as a data base (see Figure 11.1). You can sort, manipulate, and search for specific information, as you might with a data base manager program, while you are running the spreadsheet program. And *1-2-3*'s graphics capabilities are easy to use and comparable to those offered by many stand-alone programs. Most importantly, the combination of spreadsheet, data base, and graphics functions is effectively implemented, making this package a pleasure to use.

Documentation *1-2-3* comes with thorough documentation that enables readers to locate information rapidly. The package consists of a quick-reference card for the program's many functions and commands, a plastic template that slips over the function keys to identify their use, an interactive tutorial supplied on a disk, and a 356-page manual.

The manual is clearly written and includes numerous helpful illustrations. It begins with a general introduction to the program's features, followed by a section on the basic skills required to use *1-2-3*. The manual clearly states how to move the cursor, create and edit formulas, use *1-2-3* com-

A1: 'Title READY

	A	B	C	D	E	F	G	H
1	Title	Author	Price	Ordr date				
2								
3	Rocks	Stone	14.95	5/6/81				
4	Trees	Oakley	17.95	7/3/82				
5	Minerals	Silver	8.95	8/8/84				
6	Oceans	Waters	15.95	4/3/83				
7	Birds	Robin	17.95	5/5/82				
8	Mammals	Mann	14.95	6/3/81				
9	UFOs	Allyn	14.95	6/6/84				
10								
11								
12								
13								
14								
15								
16								
17								
18								
19								
20								

Figure 11.1 *A sample 1-2-3 worksheet. The box around the word "Title" indicates the cursor position.*

mands, use and name cell ranges, and create keyboard macros, a feature that enables you to program and automate the program's procedures. The second half of the manual explains how to use the program's commands to build a spreadsheet, and how to use the data base commands and graph commands, which are accessed from the spreadsheet.

The manual also includes eight appendices that explain configuring the program to your specific computer system; a reference of *1-2-3* mathematical, logical, statistical, and data base functions; and a special section that explains the use of the graph program. Also provided are lists of error messages and printer control codes, and explanations of how to use *1-2-3* with a hard disk and transfer information between programs.

The documentation also includes a glossary of computer terms and several indexes. In addition to the usual alphabetical index, Lotus offers a Functional Index that has entries keyed to major functions of the system, such as printing or graphing. There is also an index of all the commands, organized around the program's menus.

As thorough as this manual is, however, you might find that you don't need to study it to learn the program. The tutorial that Lotus includes with the program is so comprehensive and easy to follow that you could learn the fundamentals of *1-2-3* simply by completing those exercises. Packaged on a separate disk, the tutorial has four lessons on spreadsheet functions and one lesson each on the data management and graphics functions. Ultimately, using the tutorial is a faster and more natural learning method than reading the manual.

Features *1-2-3* is similar to other spreadsheets in its familiar row-and-column format. As in *VisiCalc,* rows are assigned numbers and columns are given letters, with individual cells referenced by names such as A1, B2, C10, and so on. Financial models are created by entering formulas in the cells in a manner similar to most spreadsheets.

The program's command menu, called a control panel, is displayed at the top of the screen (see Figure 11.2). Each command is represented by a word rather than a single letter, as in *VisiCalc.* Again, *1-2-3*'s command functions for copying, deleting, inserting, and formatting cells resemble those of other spreadsheets. You can also name ranges of cells and use the names in formulas. Spreadsheets can be created with lookup tables and other types of data tables.

Besides its special graphics and data base capabilities, *1-2-3* is notable for its speed of processing and its large worksheet size. It is many times faster in calculating formulas than its predecessor, *VisiCalc.* The potential size of a *1-2-3* spreadsheet is 524,288 cells, forming 256 columns and 2048 rows (if the computer's memory could store all that data). That's about equal to 882 square feet of ledger paper.

Because *1-2-3* has so many features, it is necessary to highlight some of them, rather than provide an extensive catalogue. Thus, what follows is an incomplete list of some of the more notable features of *1-2-3*. You may remember from

```
A1: 'Title                                                        READY
[Worksheet]  Range  Copy  Move  File  Print  Graph  Data  Quit
Global, Insert, Delete, Column-Width, Erase, Titles, Window, Status
      A          B           C        D         E        F        G        H
1   Title      Author      Price  Ordr date
2
3   Rocks      Stone       14.95    5/6/81
4   Trees      Oakley      17.95    7/3/82
5   Minerals   Silver       8.95    8/8/84
6   Oceans     Waters      15.95    4/3/83
7   Birds      Robin       17.95    5/5/82
8   Mammals    Mann        14.95    6/3/81
9   UFOs       Allyn       14.95    6/6/84
10
11
12
13
14
15
16
17
18
19
20
```

Figure 11.2 *The* 1-2-3 *worksheet shown in Figure 11.1 with the command lines displayed. The upper row of commands indicates major operations; the lower row indicates options available under the Worksheet command.*

Chapter 3 that *Multiplan* can display up to eight windows at once. *1-2-3* can display only two windows, but you can lock titles in place and scroll simultaneously or individually.

Although cells can be protected in *1-2-3,* you can't hide them as in *SuperCalc3*. Otherwise *1-2-3* offers all the usual options for varying column width, and formatting individual cells and ranges of cells. Cells can be formatted to display numbers in exponential (or scientific) format, as dollars, percentages, or dates, with a fixed number of decimal places, and in horizontal bar graph form.

1-2-3 has an impressive number of functions. It provides 19 mathematical functions for trigonometric calculations, logarithms, generating random numbers, rounding numbers, and finding square roots. Five logical functions offer conditional testing in a spreadsheet, and other special functions allow for the use of lookup tables, and selecting arguments from a series of choices. The program provides business users with functions that determine the internal rate of return, net present value, future value, present value, and payments over a period of time. Special date functions, which are not used in many other spreadsheets, enable formulas to include change over time.

Statistical functions are provided to determine such things as minimum and maximum values of lists of values, standard deviation, variance, and other commonly used worksheet functions. There is a problem here, however, in that the program implements two of the statistical functions, variance and standard deviation, in an unusual way. *1-2-3* uses "n" in the denominator of the variance, which yields a "population" variance, rather than "n–1," which yields a "sample" variance, statistically the more precise and preferred form. The standard deviation is biased, too, because it uses the variance in its calculations. Fortunately, the manual explains the construction of these two functions thoroughly and describes how to convert them to the preferred statistical form.

One of the great advantages of using a spreadsheet is the ability to do "what if" analyses. In this type of analysis, you change values in the worksheet and have the program recalculate the new results. *1-2-3* provides a further enhancement to this process, which enables you to create data tables showing the input and resultant values of this type of value substitution. Data tables can be created automatically using the Data Table command.

Two types of Data Table commands are available. Data Table 1 substitutes each of a series of values into a cell and creates a table based on the values of one or more dependent formulas. You can use Data Table 1 for "what if" analyses. Data Table 2 will substitute a series of values into each of two cells and create a table based on the changing values of one dependent formula. This command can be used to do "what if" analyses and to create tables for the results of statistical analyses.

One of *1-2-3*'s advanced features is its ability to automate repetitive procedures with keyboard macros. Just as you operate *1-2-3* by typing sequences of characters and commands at the keyboard, you can record these command sequences in the worksheet and implement them with a keystroke or two. For example, to print a worksheet, you may have to complete a five- or six-step procedure for selecting print options. Once set up, a keyboard macro can be used to make all the selections automatically in one swift step; unfortunately, however, setting up macros is a complex process.

You might use keyboard macros to speed up routine sequences of commands used to build parts of a worksheet, such as frequently used labels or formatting instructions. You simply enter the macro sequence in out-of-the-way cells on the worksheet and assign a two-character name to it. When you want to invoke the macro, you hold down the <Alt> key and type the macro's name. Instantly, the formatting or labeling operation is executed.

One problem with creating worksheets with such programs as *VisiCalc* and *SuperCalc* is the way the programs recalculate models. It is important to avoid creating worksheets that use forward and circular references. Programs such as *VisiCalc* and *SuperCalc* recalculate cells row by row or column by column in systematic order. If a model were created in which the result of one cell depended on another cell that was to be recalculated after it (a forward reference), the results of the recalculation would be incorrect. You might also get incorrect results if you created a model in which several cells each depended on one another (a circular reference).

1-2-3 excels at recalculation, particularly in handling forward and circular references. The program uses natural recalculation; it recalculates a formula only after it has recalculated all dependent formulas. Thus, you can use forward references without problems. If you construct a circular reference, the program will display "CIRC" on the screen.

Data base functions Data management with *1-2-3* looks different from a standard file manager or data base manager. The program's data base appears in the column-and-row worksheet format. With other types of data base managers, data is usually entered into a data entry screen, on which you see field names followed by the blanks to be filled in. Also, with a standard data base manager, you don't usually see data for more than one record at a time (unless you are constructing a special report). With *1-2-3,* however, your data base is simply part of the worksheet on the screen, and you can scroll through and review various entries like any other part of a worksheet. For example, a simple *1-2-3* data base for a customer list may appear as a block of several hundred rows filled with customer names, addresses, and other pertinent information stretching across the screen.

To build a *1-2-3* data base, you insert new rows of information in the spreadsheet. An entire row is a record, and each column represents a field for a specific type of information within the record.

Because the data base takes up space on the spreadsheet, a *1-2-3* data base can't be larger than the worksheet's capacity. So a *1-2-3* data base is limited to (and is usually smaller than) 2048 records. But a data base this size is limited. *dBASE II,* for example, can manage up to 65,000 records. Many types of data base functions, such as tracking large lists of inventory, may not be possible with a *1-2-3* data base alone.

But with *1-2-3* you can do a few things that are difficult for other file managers by using the worksheet formatting commands. For instance, you can easily add new fields or records to a data base after defining and filling it with data. And you can easily delete fields or move them. Although the data base may not have a large data capacity, it is flexible.

Like most standard data bases, *1-2-3* provides functions for searching and sorting data. Because these operations are similar in form to the other spreadsheet functions, learning them is not difficult.

With the Data Sort command you can sort records, reordering them in a specified way, usually in ascending or descending alphabetical or numerical order. You specify a range of cells to be sorted, then the type of information the sorting is based on. For example, you might sort a list of customers according to zip code. The zip code—the information you are using to reorder the records—is the primary key. You can also sort using primary and secondary keys. For example, you might sort a list of businesses by type (primary key), and within each type of business sort the individual businesses by owner's last name (secondary key). The data base would then be arranged by business type, and within each business type, records would be arranged by owner's last name.

After setting the range of records to be sorted and selecting keys, the program rearranges records into a new order on the screen. Because sorting occurs in memory (without the computer's having to read the disk to access it), *1-2-3*'s sorting is rapid.

Searching for specific information in a *1-2-3* data base is done with a Data Query command. You specify the data base to be searched, and then specify the search criterion. *1-2-3* will locate specific records by jumping the cursor directly to a record that matches your search criterion. It also extracts information from the data base (such as all customers having the last name Grant) and produces a list of the matching records in a new place on the spreadsheet. You can delete records by specifying a search criterion, and the program will erase any records that match. Although *1-2-3*'s method of setting up a search and retrieving data requires some study, you can effectively cull complex information from its data base.

Because the data base functions are so closely linked with the spreadsheet, *1-2-3* also gives you a way to analyze a data base numerically. You can use the functions Count, Sum, Average, Variation, Standard Deviation, Maximum, and Minimum to generate statistics for any given field in the data base.

The program has two other interesting data base commands: Data Fill and Data Distribution. With the Data Distribution command, you can create a frequency distribution table for a specified range of numbers. To do this, you have to specify a Bin Range, a series of ascending numbers that make up the intervals for the frequency distribution.

The program supplies the Bin Range automatically when you use the Data Fill command. You simply specify start and stop values, and the amount to increase each succeeding number, and the program assigns the actual numbers between the two values. Data Fill is also useful for creating numbered lists or labels. Data Distribution and Data Fill are not limited to the data base module of *1-2-3;* they can also be used for the spreadsheet and graphics functions.

***1-2-3* graphics** Although *1-2-3*'s graphics features are adequate, they are not outstanding compared to other graphics programs available for the PC. *1-2-3* provides graphing capabilities for five types of graphs: simple bar, stacked bar, pie, line, and X,Y. You can use up to six data series in one chart.

The program can display charts in three colors and print them in up to seven colors. Although you can add a main title and X- and Y-axis labels to a chart, there is no provision for titles in other places on the chart, and the capacity to make legends is limited.

1-2-3 can't display a worksheet and a chart on the same screen simultaneously. If you're using only an IBM Monochrome Display, you can't display a chart at all, but you can create and print one. If you're using both a monochrome monitor and a graphics monitor, *1-2-3* can show the worksheet on the monochrome unit and the charts on the graphics monitor.

To print a chart, you have to save the specifications of the graph in a graph file, leave the spreadsheet portion of the program, take out the *1-2-3* program disk, insert the disk containing the graph program, and load that program. This is one of the few awkward design features in the *1-2-3* package. Using the *PrintGraph* module, you can enlarge, reduce, or rotate your chart, and print or plot it in up to seven colors.

All in all, *1-2-3* provides basic business graphics capabilities. To be fair, however, *1-2-3* shouldn't be judged on the features of all or any one of its parts. The proof of the program is in the running, and the different applications of the program are well integrated and easy to use. Operation is natural; shortcomings in the data base and graphics functions don't seem important at all.

1-2-3 is designed specifically for the PC and the XT, and the use of the <F10> key for graphing is just one example of how this program uses all the computer's capabilities. Operations such as sorting and recalculation are fast, and the menu structure is easy to use. *1-2-3* provides a good Help facility, and you can cancel any commands before execution by pressing the <Esc> key.

The program requires a PC or an XT that has at least 192K of RAM. Although you can run the program with the IBM Monochrome Display, you will probably want a color or graphics display to view graphs before you print them. The *PrintGraph* module supports several popular dot matrix printers and plotters.

1-2-3 is an innovative program in personal computer software. Lotus's *Symphony* adds word processing, telecommunications, and enhanced data base management to the *1-2-3* package. *Symphony* promises to make the *1-2-3* implementation of multiapplication programs even better, although this enhanced program requires 320K of RAM.

PeachText 5000

PeachText 5000 is five programs packaged together: a word processor, the *Random House Electronic Thesaurus, Spelling Proofreader, List Manager,* and the *PeachCalc* electronic spreadsheet. Although a telecommunications program is also available from Peachtree, it is not included in the package. If you buy the telecommunications program, you can access it through the *PeachText 5000* main menu (see Figure 11.3).

With the exception of the unique thesaurus, the programs in *PeachText 5000* are not particularly noteworthy when considered individually. They are all adequate, but none is a standout in its application category.

Figure 11.3 *The main menu of* Peachtext 5000.

PeachText 5000 (tm) V2.02
Copyright (C) 1983 Peachtree Software Incorporated
An MSA Company

System Type: IBM PC

Default Disk: A

DOCUMENT COMMANDS
ED – Edit Document
PR – Print Document
CO – Copy Document
DE – Delete Document
RE – Rename Document
DI – Display Directory
? – Get Help!
EN – End PeachText

DISK COMMANDS
SW – Swap Disks
CW – Change Default

SPECIAL COMMANDS
SP – Spelling Proofreader
LM – List Manager
PC – PeachCalc
TC – Telecommunications

Enter Selection: __

Documentation The documentation for *PeachText 5000* is excessive and largely unsuccessful. There is a 248-page lesson plan providing tutorials, a 262-page reference guide, reference cards for the major components, and an 88-page training manual, *ATI Training Power,* accompanied by four training disks. Unfortunately, the training manual confuses the user with nonstandard terminology, such as calling a worksheet a "table" and a cell in a worksheet a "block."

Although the various manuals are full of information, the overall organization is clumsy, and it's difficult to find what you want quickly. Manuals should be organized around what you do with the program, and they should proceed logically through the program's steps. *PeachText 5000*'s manuals are organized around the program's menus, which sometimes gets in the way of natural learning.

The reference cards for the word processor and the spreadsheet are good. The Quick Start tutorial for the word processor provides such a quick start that you will have little idea what you've done when you're finished. Peachtree should improve and expand this section to include information about other parts of the program.

Word processing The central application in *PeachText 5000* is the *PeachText* word processor. Although *PeachText* has many desirable features, the program seems antiquated when compared with powerful, easy-to-use word processors such as *Microsoft Word. PeachText* is command-driven and makes minimal use of on-screen prompts and messages. You have to remember a long list of commands to get anything done, especially for formatting and printing.

With *PeachText,* what you see on the screen is not what you get on paper. To format a document, you must embed many codes within the text to control such things as margins, indentations, line spacing, and centering. Because these formatting commands do not appear on the editing screen, you do not see a final formatted version of the text until printing time. Some people may find that having to learn many formatting codes and being unable to see formatting during editing are cumbersome methods of editing text.

PeachText has good cursor control, but it doesn't always use the PC cursor keys. For scrolling, it uses the <F1> and

<F2> keys, but to move to the top or the bottom of the text, it uses <Ctrl>-T and <Ctrl>-B, rather than function keys. The <Del> key deletes a character at the cursor, <F4> deletes a word, and <F9> deletes a line. Other function keys are used for block moves and search and replace. The <Ins> key effects character insertion at the cursor position, and <F8> makes larger insertions.

PeachText is an adequate document editor, but it lacks the sophistication of programs such as *Word, WordStar,* and *MultiMate*. This lack of sophistication in advanced text formatting, cursor movement, and block marking, as well as the lack of special text entry procedures such as macros, make *PeachText* more difficult to use and less efficient than other programs.

PeachText has one very desirable feature: it enables you to merge print documents for mass mailings. You insert variable names into a document, and then substitute actual values for the variables during printing. Although this is a valuable feature, the procedure for using variables is complicated. To fill in the variable values, you either have to sit at the keyboard and enter the values one by one as the program prompts you, or set up a data file with the values and instruct the program to "fill in the blanks" from the data file automatically. To use a data file for variables, you have to write a short program, a process that seems needlessly complex.

Although *PeachText* lacks a "Window" feature, you can switch among documents on the screen without leaving the Edit mode. By using the Display command from the main menu, you display the first screen of any document on your data disk. You can then page through the document and find passages that you might want to include in the current document. When you're finished perusing the second document, you can return to the current one through the main menu.

Once you create a document with the editor, you switch to the printing portion of the program to finalize formatting and printing specifications. A print menu is used initially to set such parameters as page length, top and bottom margins, left and right margins, indentations, line spacing, and lines per inch. You can enter or change these variables before printing or embed the corresponding format codes in text; these codes then override the menu parameters.

You can print all or part of a document, print a document to disk, or view the formatted document on the screen. Depending on the capabilities of the printer, you can use proportional spacing. You can print text left, right, or fully justified, with underlining, boldfacing, superscripts, subscripts, soft hyphens, and hard spaces. *PeachText* also provides print spooling, which enables you to print a document while editing another. The program can produce templates for standard correspondence and integrate boilerplate paragraphs into form letters or contracts. You can enter the filler data either from the keyboard or from data files. You can also create custom files to help with difficult procedures.

Although adequate as a word processor, *PeachText* seems dated. A couple of years ago its features would have been impressive, but it doesn't compare favorably with other word processors currently on the market. Because it is the centerpiece of *PeachText 5000,* you might expect it to be more impressive.

Thesaurus In contrast, the *Random House Electronic Thesaurus* is impressive. It can generate a total of 26,000 synonyms for 4400 key words. You use the thesaurus when editing a document with *PeachText.* To see the synonyms for a word, you simply put the cursor on the first letter of the target word and press the <F10> key. If there are more synonyms than can be displayed on the screen, you scroll through the synonym list. As you move from synonym to synonym, a set of brackets encloses each word. When the brackets enclose the word you want, press <Enter>, and the thesaurus replaces the target word with the chosen synonym.

The process for substituting words is very efficient, but if you have not installed the thesaurus program on your *PeachText* disk, you will have to load the thesaurus disk separately and replace it with the *PeachText* disk when you finish. This is an example of the lack of direct integration in the *PeachText 5000* package.

Spelling checker The *PeachText 5000* spelling checker program checks the spelling of every word in a document, displays misspelled words, and marks them for correction.

The program will neither suggest alternate spellings nor display misspelled words in the context of surrounding text. You can, however, create a custom dictionary to include specialized vocabulary.

You also have to do a disk shuffle to use *Spelling Proofreader.* Although the spelling checker has some desirable features, its standard dictionary contains about 20,000 words, which is small by current standards. You can add words to the main dictionary, buy specialized dictionaries from Peachtree, or create specialized dictionaries of your own.

Although nothing is especially noteworthy about the way *Spelling Proofreader* works, the program features good displays that report what is going on. For instance, the Spell Check Document screen tells you the number of words read, the number of words that are unique, the percentage of unique words, the number of words misspelled (those that don't match dictionary entries), the percentage of words misspelled, and the percentage of proofing done.

The spelling checker enables you to review words that may be misspelled. Each word is displayed individually, and you can decide whether it needs correction or should be added to the dictionary. Once the program has been run and misspelled words marked, you must reedit the document with the *PeachText* editor to make corrections.

List Manager *List Manager* is a simple file management program whose real strength is setting up mailing lists for *PeachText* files. Each file can have up to 32,765 records, and each record can accommodate up to 14 fields. The program will sort on a primary key and two secondary keys, in ascending or descending order.

You can either print reports directly from *List Manager* or create data files for use with *PeachText.* If you want to get the most out of integration from *PeachText 5000,* you should use *List Manager* in conjunction with the word processor, but the procedure for creating data files for use in *PeachText* form letters is cumbersome and complex—another example of poor integration.

Spreadsheet Although *PeachCalc,* the electronic spreadsheet in *PeachText 5000,* is an adequate spreadsheet, it has little if any direct integration with the word processing module. You can prepare a *PeachCalc* file and insert it into a *PeachText* document, but you cannot switch directly from word processing to spreadsheet operations.

Although the spreadsheet is not integrated with the other parts of *PeachText 5000,* it is adequate. With 63 columns and 254 rows, *PeachCalc* can handle any routine spreadsheet job. The number of built-in functions is limited, however; no date functions are available, and the only business function is net present value. Although *PeachCalc* does offer the use of lookup tables, you can't use text in them.

PeachCalc has good formatting features. You can vary the width of individual columns, text entries can spill over into empty, adjacent columns, and entries can be protected. The program supports two windows, which can be scrolled independently. Titles and labels can be locked into place. You can combine worksheets, and you can print the entire worksheet or parts of it.

Probably the best feature of the program is its ease of use. Commands are kept to a minimum, and the screen display has lots of useful information, such as the amount of memory available, the current cursor direction, the location of the bottom of your worksheet, and so on. Error messages are nontechnical and relatively clear, and on-line help is always available. *PeachCalc* is not particularly powerful, but it is not difficult to use. The major drawback is that the spreadsheet in *PeachText 5000* isn't directly integrated with the word processing application.

Support Although Peachtree offers an excellent one-year support plan for *PeachText 5000,* you have to pay $96 for it. A free 90-day assistance plan gives you a technical support phone number to call. If you want access to a toll-free number and the opportunity to upgrade your software at reduced prices, you have to buy the one-year plan.

PeachText 5000 is unimpressive as an integrated package. Because the level of direct integration is low and none of the individual programs is exceptional in its own right, you could do better by assembling your own package, made up of outstanding individual programs for the PC and the XT. Or better yet, use one of the new operating environments, such as *Windows* or *DesQ,* to bundle outstanding individual programs in a truly integrated and powerful framework.

Visi On

Visi On (VisiCorp) was the first operating environment to be announced, but it took a long time to reach dealers' shelves. Even though the wait for *Visi On* was a long one, the product itself is powerful and polished and performs as originally advertised.

The *Visi On* system is built around the *Applications Manager,* a program that provides the actual framework, or environment, for the applications software, such as a word processing program or electronic spreadsheet. This operating environment features a mouse for moving a pointer on the screen, for invoking commands, and for scrolling; windows, or screen divisions, for viewing the output from different applications programs; and extensive menus of commands.

Some observers have criticized VisiCorp for not designing *Visi On* to accept programs from other manufacturers without modification, as do some other operating environments. While this approach does limit the choices of available applications, the programs that VisiCorp has furnished for the *Visi On* system are first rate. And because they are designed expressly for the *Visi On* environment, the programs' similar command structure, menu choices, and operating syntax significantly shorten the learning process.

The Applications Manager Because the *Visi On* system is so complex, it requires an XT with 512K of RAM, or a PC with 512K of RAM and a 10-megabyte hard disk. Before you can use the system, you must install the individual programs, which are furnished on separate floppy disks, on the hard disk. The procedure for installation is straightforward, and the operator's manual has clear instructions that are easy to follow.

Once the programs reside on your hard disk, it is a simple matter to call the system into action. After startup, the system will display the *Visi On* Global Menu and the Services screen. The Global Menu displays eight commands, which are the basic operating instructions for the *Visi On* system. The first global command is Help. Selecting this command puts extensive, context-sensitive help screens at your disposal.

Three other global commands—Open, Full, and Frame—are also used to manipulate windows. The Open command creates a new window. By selecting the Full command and designating a window, you cause that window to fill the entire screen. With the Frame command, you can actually draw a window to any size and in any position by using the pointer. The Close command closes a window when you are through using it, and stores the contents of the window for future use.

The Options command is one of the richest features of the *Visi On* system. You use this command to set the display characteristics of information in any given window. By selecting the Options command, you cause an Options sheet to appear in the right side of the active window. Using the pointer, you can set and reset the display characteristics, such as line spacing in a document or column width in a worksheet. The program will retain your option selections and save them with your program.

The Transfer command allows you to move data from one window to another and from one application to another. The ability to transfer data between applications is one of the most important benefits of an operating environment, and *Visi On* has implemented this critical feature very well. Transferring data is especially useful for consolidating spreadsheets, graphing data from spreadsheets, and including spreadsheet calculations and graphs in written reports.

The procedure itself is similar to a block move in a word processing program. You first select the Transfer command and the window with the material to be moved. The program prompts you to mark the beginning and end points of the material, then highlights your choice so you are sure that what you see is what gets moved. You are then prompted to mark the window and the beginning point in that window where the material will be moved. When you finish the command, the data is moved quickly and precisely to the desired location. There are restrictions on the kinds of data that can be transferred between certain applications, but *Visi On* will prevent you from making any fatal errors.

The Services Window is the first screen you will see after starting the *Visi On* system. Although it has seven menu choices, you will use it primarily for starting *Visi On* applications. The second menu choice, Install, is used for putting new *Visi On* applications on the hard disk. When you select Start, the program will ask which applications you want, and you then select one of the four *Visi On* applications: *Calc, Graph, Query,* or *Word. Visi On Query,* the data base program, is not discussed here.

The Visi On desktop The *Visi On* system simulates a desktop. You use the mouse to shuffle papers on the desk and to add and remove papers. The electronic access to a document is through a window on the screen. When you open a window, it becomes the active window and overlays any other windows that were previously on the screen. If you want to designate a new active window from those currently on the screen, you just select it with the mouse, and it moves to the top of the pile. Selecting is accomplished by placing the mouse pointer on an object on the screen and pressing the left button on the mouse.

You can change the shape and location of any window by using the Frame command. When you close a window it doesn't just disappear. *Visi On* stores the window and displays a list of stored windows in a small box in the upper right corner of the screen.

Usually a window shows only a part of a document or file. To see all the information, you must use *Visi On*'s scrolling feature, which is controlled by the mouse. You place the mouse pointer in the area you want to scroll, and press the right button. You will see the pointer change shape to resemble a diamond with a cross in it. You then move the mouse in the direction you want the material to move. *Visi On* has several scrolling speeds, and you can choose your speed by the distance you move the mouse on the pad. Use of the mouse for scrolling becomes second nature quickly, and it is a very fast method for moving through documents.

The *Visi On* filing system lets you organize your documents into folders. You access this filing sytem by selecting the File menu item from any of the applications programs. Once into the file system, you can create new folders, get ones you have already used, and perform document-handling operations. This filing system is used for all the *Visi On* applications.

Visi On Calc Anyone who has used a version of *Visi-Calc* will feel very much at home with *Visi On Calc.* It is similar to the latest version of VisiCalc, but the *Visi On* environment makes all the difference in terms of speed and flexibility. The *Visi On Calc* screen has four lines of information at the bottom. The bottom line is the *Visi On* global menu, and the second line up contains the *Calc* menu, with ten choices. The third line up is the Prompt line, which displays program messages that direct you through the necessary actions. The top line is called the "echo" line; it contains information about the contents of the active cell in a worksheet.

The *Calc* menu has ten items, five of which begin with capital letters. Of course, you can invoke any command with the mouse, but you can also use the keyboard to make any commands that begin with a lowercase letter. You do this by pressing <Esc>, the first letter of the command, and <Enter>.

One of the first things you notice about *Visi On Calc* is the ease and speed of cursor control with the mouse. For moving the cursor within the current window, you simply move the pointer to the desired cell and select it. The program tells you which cell the pointer is in at any time by highlighting the appropriate column and row coordinates. You can use the cursor keys to move the cursor, too, but the mouse is much faster. For moving to a distant part of the worksheet, there is a GoTo command.

Visi On Calc offers several convenient ways of entering labels in the worksheet. As with other spreadsheet programs, you can enter numbers as labels by preceding them with a single quotation mark, and the program automatically treats any entry that begins with an alphabetic character as a label. But *Calc* also has a Label command. With this command, anything you enter in a cell will be interpreted as a label. When you use the label command, the program goes into a "power entry" mode, in which the cursor automatically moves to a designated cell after you type your label. The default power entry is for the cursor to move down to the next cell in a column, but you can set it to move one cell to the right in a row or to a preset location.

It is especially easy with *Visi On Calc* to change the display characteristics of a worksheet by using options sheets.

When you select the Attributes command, an attributes options sheet appears on the right side of the *Calc* screen. You can then scroll through the sheet until you find the characteristic you want to change. You don't have to remember a complex series of commands, because everything is visible to you. All you have to do is use the mouse to select the changes you want to make, and the worksheet is automatically reformatted.

Considered alone, *Visi On Calc* is certainly not a breakthrough product. Most of its features can be found in other good spreadsheets. But the *Visi On* system features, which impart speed and ease of operation to the *Calc* program, make this application an outstanding performer. And the true value of *Calc* becomes apparent when used with the other *Visi On* applications as part of a system.

Visi On Graph The *Graph* application is a straightforward program that emphasizes convenience and speed rather than features. It offers an adequate range of features, but does not provide a lot of bells and whistles. For instance, the program has no time series analysis features.

The procedures for building a graph are standard, too. First, you enter the data series that you want to graph, or—more likely with *Visi On*—you transfer the data from another *Visi On* application, such as *Calc*. Next, you select the type of graph you want. Then you draw the graph, adding all the extras such as titles, legends, markers, and so forth. Finally, you print the graph, or you might choose to transfer it to another *Visi On* application, such as *Visi On Word*.

While *Graph* is similar to VisiCorp's standard graphics program, *VisiPlot,* it is much richer. You can choose from among bar, pie, line, area, high-low-close, and *X,Y* graphs. Bar charts can be stacked or positioned side-by-side for comparison. Several different point markers are available. The program can also overlay one type of graph on another.

Creating and moving titles is quite simple with *Visi On Graph*. Titles can be entered at both the bottom and the top of a graph; labels can be placed anywhere on the graph. You use the pointer and mouse to move labels, and you can preview prospective label locations before you actually make the move. Several type fonts are available for labels and titles as well.

You can also preview a graph before you print it, and the program will display the graph on screen in exactly the size it will be printed. You can use the options command to add niceties such as borders or grid marks. The program will support up to 12 colors and will print on paper as large as 11 by 17 inches. A full range of popular printers and plotters are supported.

Visi On Word This application is based on VisiCorp's excellent word processing program, *VisiWord. Visi On Word* adds the mouse-controlled pointer to the old *VisiWord,* making cursor movement fast and powerful.

While mouse control may be great for "cut-and-paste" editing, it is not as efficient for entering text. For this reason, all the commands in *Visi On Word* can be invoked from the keyboard as well as with the mouse, including cursor control. To enter a command from the keyboard, you press <Esc> and the first letter of the command.

The *Visi On Word* editing screen is rather more complex. At the top of the screen is a status line, which tells you what mode you are in (insert or overtype), the page and line where the cursor is positioned, the name of your document, and whether any special character attributes, such as italics, are in force. If you are using italics, boldface, or underlining, the word "Text" on the status line is displayed in the appropriate style. The second line on the screen is a ruler that displays tab stops and margins, which you can easily change. The program's basic commands are displayed on the bottom of the edit screen.

The PC's function keys control many of the program's special character attributes. As an alternative to the function keys, you can use the options sheet to determine how you enter text, how the program displays text, and how your edit screen is configured. When you use the Options command, the sheet appears on the right side of the screen so you can scroll through all your choices and select what you want. For instance, you might want to italicize a sentence or change the line spacing after you have finished your document. You can do this with the options sheet and save your changes if you wish.

Visi On Word is also outstanding in its display of text. It shows your document just as it will be printed, including such attributes as boldface and underlining. And, of course, with *Visi On*'s multiple windows, it is easy to make block moves within long documents and to inspect different parts of a document quickly.

A good investment The *Visi On* system is a well crafted and powerful operating environment. The documentation is superb, and the system works with no major flaws. Currently only four applications are available, although these programs cover the standard business needs rather well. A lot of hardware is required to run the system, too, and it is relatively expensive. Even with the expense and the limited choice of software, however, *Visi On* delivers state-of-the-art performance in a convenient, high-quality package.

CHAPTER TWELVE

Accounting

Because accounting is such a basic, universal business function, accounting programs have been around for a long time in mainframe and minicomputer versions. Accounting software for the PC is also well established, and the introduction of the XT, with its large data storage capacity, has inspired software developers to adapt large, complex integrated accounting systems from the minicomputer environment.

Bookkeeping is an ideal application for computers. There are strict rules that govern keeping accounting records, and the entry and maintenance of accounting books tend to be repetitive and tedious. By using a PC or an XT and accounting software, a professional or small-business owner can avoid tedium and save time and money while maintaining first-class business records.

Accounting programs are usually modular in nature, providing separate components for such operations as general ledger, accounts payable, accounts receivable, and payroll. Most software firms sell the components individually, although some offer useful, though less comprehensive, all-in-one accounting packages.

You can often use individual parts of an integrated system as stand-alone applications and even copy their results into your other uncomputerized accounting records. You can also use two or more modules together as an interactive package. Usually the more parts of a system you use, the more a computerized accounting system benefits you in both time and cost. If your business does not need a complete integrated accounting system, you can probably do well with one or two accounting modules.

Accounting Modules

The four major components that make up most accounting systems are general ledger, accounts receivable, accounts payable, and payroll. The first and most important part is the general ledger, or general accounting, module. This is the hub into which all the other parts feed data. Many businesses get along well with only a general ledger program. Other modules have considerable power, however, and include an accounts receivable program that tracks customer transactions. Accounts payable records payments to suppliers. A payroll module provides an accounting of payments to employees. You can generally use any one of these four programs by itself, but together they form a basic interactive package.

Three other components are usually offered as part of more sophisticated accounting systems: inventory, sales orders, and job costing. Inventory programs keep track of the inventory you have in stock and the value of that inventory. Sales order packages are subsidiary programs of accounts receivable. They track sales activity by customer and exchange resulting information with related accounting programs. Job costing programs use data from other accounting modules to track the expenditures and revenues associated with individual projects or jobs. These programs produce the same kind of data as some stand-alone project management programs available for the PC.

General ledger The general ledger program is the cornerstone of any accounting system. It documents the total financial activity of a business during a given accounting period. General ledger programs are designed to record all financial transactions and keep an up-to-date balance of those transactions for various accounts.

Report production is another important function of the general ledger. Any general ledger program provides three basic reports. The trial balance report represents an initial accounting of all transactions for a given period. The balance sheet is a summary of a company's assets, liabilities, and owner's equity. The income statement summarizes income, expenses, and profit or loss of a business for a given period (this report is sometimes called the profit and loss statement). Some programs produce departmental income statements if needed.

Another important function of the general ledger is to provide comparisons of current results with results from an earlier period. This comparative data is not only useful for gauging how well a business is doing, but also provides information vital for managing a company's finances.

Accounts receivable Managing accounts receivable is crucial to the financial health of a business, and computer-based accounts receivable programs take the guesswork out of the process. Accounts receivable programs keep track of all information dealing with customer transactions and payments. These programs enable you to check a customer's last payment and last order, outstanding balance, and the "age" of purchases made on credit. Having obtained this information, you might decide to cut off credit for tardy payers or extend extra credit to the best customers. The accounts receivable program also enables you to design and produce invoices. The information processed by this module is automatically shared with other related accounting programs if you are using an integrated system.

Accounts payable Accounts payable helps manage cash flow. An accounts payable program provides information that you can use to keep from paying creditors too much too soon. These programs can produce a complete record for each vendor that shows how much you have already paid and how much you owe. The program automatically keeps track of any credits or discounts owed to you, as well as intervals of installments. Some programs automatically screen a list of payments due and select the most advantageous mix of creditors to pay. Accounts payable programs can even be used to print checks and serve as check registers.

Payroll A payroll program keeps track of all expenses associated with employees. Payroll programs track salaries, wage rates, withholding data, vacation time, and sick leave. More advanced systems accommodate data on tips, commissions, pension plans, local taxes, and other specific information. Payroll programs can produce reports for payroll registers, earnings records, tax information, check registers, and other relevant data. These programs can also produce W-2 forms at tax time and other forms related to federal, state, or local taxes. Some payroll programs are so flexible they can create tax tables for the state and locality of your specific business.

Inventory control A computerized inventory system can help ensure that you have important inventory in stock. These programs enable you to code inventory items in several different ways, including by item number, location, and price. At the most basic level, the program keeps track of what you have on hand, what is committed to sales orders, and what is on order.

More advanced inventory programs help in reordering stock by alerting you to low inventory levels for a given product. Although several methods of valuation can be used for inventory, depending on the accounting method you choose, the best programs offer the flexibility to adapt inventory records to the patterns of specific business operations.

Basic reports produced by an inventory program include a status of each inventory item, sales by item, a master price list, and an inventory adjustments listing. Advanced reports offered by some programs include sales analyses of inventory items to help judge turnover. Such a report can be a big help in budgeting and forecasting your buying.

Sales order programs Not a critical part of most accounting systems, but a module that is good to have, is a sales invoicing program. If you are also using an inventory program, a sales program can often automatically earmark inventory for a particular order, put stock on back order if none is available, and commit stock on order to the appropriate sales invoice.

With these programs, you can often relate sales to several other accounting areas for better analysis and planning.

For example, you may be able to generate reports of sales by territory, salesperson, customer, product, and so on. These programs usually automatically compute taxes and freight charges and may even check on the ordering customer's available credit. Sales reports include sales order and outstanding order lists, and some programs enable you to specify your own report formats. A few programs even produce confirmations of orders for mailing to customers.

Job cost programs Job cost packages are especially useful for a company that has to manage several complex projects and allocate costs among them. Attorneys, contractors, and consultants have businesses that could make good use of these programs. Job cost programs allocate direct labor and materials costs to projects, and some of the advanced programs can even allocate overhead based on several measures, such as hours or dollars.

Choosing a Modular Accounting System

As noted previously, general ledger, accounts receivable, accounts payable, and payroll programs can usually be purchased and used as independent accounting applications. With the latter three applications, you might find that using them independently is difficult, because they are most often designed to share information with other accounting modules. Without the other related parts of the system, an independent module might not be most efficient to use, because it can't be updated automatically and accessed by other parts of an accounting system. You will generally benefit most from an accounting application if you use the entire system.

The modular nature of accounting software calls for a buying strategy that is different from what you might use for a stand-alone program. The major difference is that you want a flexible accounting system that can grow with your business. Rather than buying a complete, basic system of several applications, you might want to start with the general ledger module of a larger, more sophisticated system and computerize your accounting gradually with a system that can handle more complex tasks as your business grows.

Because you will be entering a large amount of data into an accounting system daily, and because you need to stay with the same system over time to realize the benefits of integration and shared data, you will find that your business will become "hooked" on whatever system you start with. Switching one computerized accounting system over to another completely different one is a huge task. You therefore want to select an efficient, capable accounting package that you'll be satisfied with for a long time.

As an additional precaution, and to ensure that things are running smoothly, you may want to maintain a manual backup system when you first begin using a computer-based accounting system. Operate both systems until you are satisfied that the computer program is handling things properly.

Accounting Program Features

Because an accounting program is basically a data base management system, the structure and features of these two types of applications are similar. Let's take a look at a general ledger program to see exactly how an accounting package works and what its features are.

If you were to draw a program "map" of a general ledger program, it would look like a *Y*, a main stem with two branches. One branch maintains the chart of accounts, or permanent accounting files, and the other branch handles data entry, or new transactions. The two branches combine to form the central program, which produces the trial balance and reports such as the balance sheet and income statement. The data query and report functions of a general ledger program are similar to those of any data base management system. If you are using the general ledger as part of an interactive accounting system, a subprogram usually transfers data from the general ledger to the various accounting applications.

Another way in which accounting software resembles data base management is in the need to define an accounting structure. You can't just load an accounting program into your PC and start computing. First you have to define a chart of accounts for your business. This process is like defining the records and the fields of a data base. Once you have established the chart of accounts, which is maintained in the master file, you can add or delete accounts and edit the information in any individual account.

Capabilities differ among accounting programs for the

number of accounts that can be maintained in a master file. The number of transactions that you can process is usually limited by the amount of disk storage available. A typical maximum for accounts is 800. If you were using a PC that had two floppy disk drives and you had 300 accounts in the master file, you would have room for about 600 transactions on the same disk. The more accounts you have, the fewer transactions you can accommodate. You can see that for a business that has any volume of transactions, an XT or a PC with a hard disk is preferable.

Using the System

System initialization is the first step in setting up the general ledger program. It consists of entering basic information, such as your company's name and address, into the program, establishing the parameters of the accounting system, such as account number ranges and months of the fiscal year, and installing the other accounting programs you might be using with the general ledger.

Because it is very important in accounting to date transactions and reports, programs usually have a separate menu item for entering the data into the computer system. The first order of business is generally setting the date.

Next, you must build a master account file. To enter an account into the master file, you simply follow the program's prompts field by field. The first field will be the account number, which you supply; the first three digits generally represent the major account, and the fourth and fifth digits represent a subaccount or departmental code. Most programs contain some standard fields, such as the account description and type, for which you supply data, and the current balance and year-to-date amounts, which are calculated by the program. Some programs let you set up additional fields, such as one to compare current monthly amounts with the previous year's figures.

Because accounting programs are so closely and extensively interrelated when used as a system, you must enter data carefully. Any incorrect entry will flow through the system like a bad penny, affecting data throughout the system. Although there are ways to correct bad data once it's in the system, they are not nearly as easy as getting it right in the first place. Just about anyone in business can tell horror stories about incorrect data spreading far and wide through a complex accounting system.

In addition to entering the basic account data when initiating your computer accounting system, you can use the master file's maintenance program to delete accounts or add new ones at a later date. This same maintenance program is used to query the master file on individual accounts. For example, you can use it to produce a report on the accounts in the master file, showing current account status or just listing the chart of accounts.

Once you have set up a chart of accounts in the master file, the majority of the accounting work involves entering daily transactions. Data entry is usually simple, but because there are often many codes to assign, you must be careful to enter the right information. You can easily change incorrect data while you are entering it, but once you have entered it and quit the transactions entry program, you can't change it.

There are two ways to correct an improper entry once it has been recorded. The first and best way is to enter a balancing transaction with an opposite dollar amount. If you make an incorrect entry for $100, for example, you can cancel it by entering a negative $100 and then entering the correct figure. Your second option is to delete the incorrect transaction, but because it creates problems in establishing an audit trail, that option is not recommended.

To help you check the transactions you have made, most programs produce a control report that provides a list on the screen of all the transactions entered. (Some programs will also print out this list.) The program then automatically edits your transactions to conform with your account definition and, if everything checks out, updates all the accounts in the master file with the latest information. Any rejected transactions are usually displayed on the screen.

When using some general ledger programs, you have to make two entries for every transaction, while other programs automatically make the second entry. Under any accrual accounting system, for example, double entries are required to keep accounts in balance. The two types of entries are a debit and a credit. For every debit there must be an offsetting credit; the general ledger program accomplishes this by representing debits as positive numbers and credits as negative entries at the time of transaction entry.

Increases and decreases in various types of accounts are represented by debits and credits. For instance, an increase in an asset account is shown by a debit, and a decrease is represented by a credit. Liability and capital accounts are just the opposite—a debit for a decrease and a credit for an increase. Sales accounts are handled like liabilities, and expense accounts are dealt with just as assets are.

A typical transaction might be the purchase of a piece of equipment for $100 from a vendor. To make the entry, you would credit your cash account for $100 and debit the equipment account for $100. If you bought the equipment on credit, you would debit the equipment account and credit a liability account. Most programs don't print out negative numbers on the balance sheet and income statements for accounts that normally carry a negative balance, unless the account is actually showing negative results for the period.

All the transactions for a given period accumulate in a transactions file, and the program can print out reports of all the entries in the file, or specific entries by source code. You can also get a listing of any individual account and all the transactions posted to that account for the current period. Either of these reports can usually be viewed on screen or printed on paper.

Information in the transaction and master list files are combined and updated monthly by a trial balance module. This subprogram matches each account with its transactions, makes sure the accounts balance, and updates the master file by transferring transaction totals to current amount totals. The trial balance report lists each account and all its transactions for the month.

Three other basic reports that a general ledger program can produce are the balance sheet, the income statement, and the departmental income statement. You can print any of these reports monthly or annually. If you like, you can usually have comparative data from the previous year printed on the same report. On the income statements, both consolidated and departmental, you can also include amounts budgeted for each account, so you can track actual versus budgeted expenses during the year.

A general ledger program's end-of-period processing routine clears the current period's data, updates it to the accounts, and sets up blank files for new data. This kind of summarizing can be done monthly or at the end of the fiscal year. The program reviews all the accounts and erases all the previous transactions. Most programs require that you back up the current transactions before erasing them.

Some accounting programs, usually the biggest and most complex, have optional report writers similar to those of data base management systems. These add-on reporting programs extend reporting capabilities and sometimes produce data in a form that can be transferred directly to other software, such as spreadsheets or data base managers. This electronic transfer feature is very valuable, because accounting data is so useful for other applications. Financial data is the most basic and important information required for budgeting, managing daily business, planning, investing, and just about any other business function. A computerized, fully integrated accounting system puts critical data at your fingertips daily.

Although it might seem that automating an accounting system means that you would need fewer people to maintain the system, that is not necessarily true. The PC or the XT, however, will free an accounting staff from tedious, mechanical bookkeeping, so that they can concentrate on accounting and other important financial functions. It might also seem that you would not need an outside accountant if you do your own books on the PC. But you will probably want to keep the services of your accountant even if you keep your own records. Accountants provide many valuable services that have little to do with bookkeeping, not the least of which is good advice.

Special Hardware Requirements

There are a few special hardware requirements for accounting software. You will probably want a 132-column printer, although you can get by with an 80-column printer in compressed mode. Although the minimum system you will need is two floppy disk drives and 64K of RAM, you will find that more internal memory and a hard disk make accounting much easier. In fact, the XT, with its larger storage capacity, is the ideal computer for accounting applications, especially if you are using an integrated system. If you use all the parts of some of the largest systems, you could be using as many as 16 program disks (unless you had a hard disk).

In general, accounting programs tend to have the same problems as data base management systems. They can be very slow in executing certain operations and can be difficult to learn and use. But given the repetitive and relatively stable nature of the accounting function, these programs are usually efficient once you learn them. Accounting on the PC or the XT is an excellent business application.

CHAPTER THIRTEEN

An Introduction to Peachpak 4 and BPI Systems

Large, integrated accounting systems have been available for personal computers for only a few years, because previously the capabilities and data storage capacities of the hardware had been limited. But the IBM PC, and particularly the XT, can now support sophisticated accounting systems easily, and many are being adapted from larger computers to run on smaller machines.

Two of the most popular accounting systems for the PC and the XT are *Peachpak 4* (Peachtree Software) and the accounting programs from BPI Systems, Inc. The *Peachpak 4* system introduced in this chapter includes general ledger, accounts receivable, and accounts payable. The BPI programs include general ledger, accounts receivable, accounts payable, and payroll.

Peachpak 4

Peachpak 4 is a good starter system for a small business that is just beginning to computerize its accounting. Although the capacity of its general ledger program is somewhat limited and the overall system doesn't have the fancy features of some larger systems, it is adequate and reliable. And if your business outgrows the *Peachpak 4* system, Peachtree has a full line of more advanced accounting programs that form a complete, interactive system.

Documentation The documentation for each *Peachpak 4* program is excellent and is especially appropriate for novices. Each manual begins with an overview that explains the purpose of the program, presents a map of the program and describes how the program is designed, and lays out the required equipment and program capacities. An operator's guide takes you through the menu step by step, and a Special Aids section explains important parts of the program in detail. The only items lacking are a detailed table of contents and an index, but the manuals are so short and the organization so obvious that you can usually find what you want quickly. The writing is clear and defines accounting terms for novices.

General ledger The hub of the *Peachpak 4* system is the general ledger program, which provides basic and advanced features. This is where the chart of accounts is established.

Setting up a chart of accounts is one of the most important steps in automating an accounting system. Peachtree's method of defining accounts offers flexibility in adapting an existing, manual system to a computer (see Figure 13.1). All accounts are identified with five-digit codes. The first three digits represent the main account, and the last two identify departmental or subsidiary accounts—up to 99 departmental accounts. Account descriptions can be up to 25 characters long. *Peachpak 4* offers nine types of accounts, including titling, posting, and totaling.

Although entering transactions into the *Peachpak 4* general ledger is not difficult, all data must be in double-entry form. For anyone who has maintained a manual accounting system, which is usually double-entry, this should not be a problem. You can define up to eight source codes for entering transactions, and the program can accommodate a single transaction up to $9,999,999. If you are using the *Peachpak 4* accounts payable and accounts receivable programs, they automatically post transactions to the general ledger.

```
PEACHTREE SOFTWARE
GENERAL LEDGER  -  00000000000  -  V2.000
COPYRIGHT 1978-1982 PEACHTREE SOFTWARE INCORPORATED
PROGRAM SELECTION MENU
--------------------------------------------------
YOU MAY SELECT ANY OF THE FOLLOWING PROGRAMS:

DA    SET TODAY'S DATE
MF    MASTER FILE MAINTENANCE
ET    ENTER DAILY TRANSACTIONS
AT    ACCOUNTING TRANSFER
RP    FINANCIAL REPORTING (SUBMENU)
EP    END OF PERIOD PROCESSING
ML    MASTER FILE LIST
TL    TRANSACTION FILE LIST
DT    DELETE A TRANSACTION
QA    QUERY ACCOUNT STATUS
SI    SYSTEM INITIALIZATION
END   END SYSTEM SELECT

WHICH PROGRAM DO YOU WISH TO SELECT? __
```

Figure 13.1 *The opening menu for* Peachpak 4, *showing the program's simplicity of operation.*

Peachpak 4's general ledger produces a good set of basic financial reports. The balance sheet is a summary report of the status of asset, liability, and equity accounts (see Figure 13.2). You can either print information for the current period only or add comparative information from a previous year. You can also create subsidiary schedules.

Probably the most useful report for a business is the income statement. With the *Peachpak 4* general ledger program, you can create an income statement for an entire business or for individual departments. You can also have the report with or without comparative information for previous years. And because the program also includes information about how much you have budgeted for each income statement item, you can keep track of your monthly expenditures and revenues.

You can also set up the general ledger to include a column for Income Ratio on the income statement. This ratio

TAYLOR OFFICE EQUIPMENT PAGE 1
GENERAL LEDGER
BALANCE SHEET
06/08/84

ASSETS

CASH	$2,920.77		
ACCOUNTS RECEIVABLE	$37,441.45		
PREPAID EXPENSES	$490.00		
INVENTORY	$13,853.79		
TOTAL CURRENT ASSETS		$54,706.01	
FURNITURE & EQUIPMENT	$4,255.37		
ACCUMULATED DEPRECIATION	$966.40 –		
DEPOSITS	$750.00		
TOTAL FIXED ASSETS		$4,038.97	
TOTAL ASSETS			$58,744.98
			=======

LIABILITIES & CAPITAL

ACCOUNTS PAYABLE	$14,410.14		
TAXES PAYABLE	$3,963.68		
TOTAL CURR LIABILITIES		$18,373.82	
NOTE PAYABLE-BANK	$600.00		
TOTAL-LONG TERM LIAB.		$600.00	
TOTAL LIABILITIES			$18,973.82
CAPITAL STOCK		$25,000.00	
RETAINED EARNINGS		$8,773.26	
CURRENT EARNINGS		$5,997.90	
TOTAL CAPITAL			$39,771.16
TOTAL LIAB. & CAPITAL			$58,744.98
			=======

Figure 13.2 *Opposite: A sample balance sheet produced with* Peachpak 4.

measures the percent of net sales for such items as gross profit, all expense items, and net income. These ratios provide useful statistics for cost analysis.

Peachpak 4 produces several other general ledger reports, including a trial balance, an examination of individual account status, a transactions register, a list of the chart of accounts, two kinds of transaction control reports, and a transfer summary journals control report that shows what has been transferred automatically from the payables or receivables programs.

The *Peachpak 4* general ledger does not have great data storage or access capacities. Within the chart of accounts, the program can accommodate about 800 accounts. The number of transactions is limited by the storage space available on disk after you have created the chart of accounts. In other words, because accounts and transactions vie for the same space on the disk, if you're trying to run your system on floppy disks, the total amount possible for one double-sided disk is about 1800. If you have 300 accounts, you can have about 1200 transactions. Obviously, an XT with a 10-megabyte hard disk has more than adequate room for storing transaction data.

Accounts receivable It's imperative for any business to take in payments as quickly as possible when goods are sold. *Peachpak 4*'s accounts receivable program can help you do this by providing up-to-date information on your customers' accounts and preparing the necessary bills to generate cash flow. It can be used either separately or with the general ledger program. In addition to keeping internal accounting records, the accounts receivable module can produce invoices and statements with sales or dunning messages for your customers.

Accounts receivable provides a customer file that contains permanent information about each customer, as well as information about a customer's ongoing payment and credit record. The program automatically updates the customer's payment and credit information, including date and amount of last debit, date and amount of last credit, year-to-date sales, and year-to-date payments. The program also records other permanent information, including company name, address, phone number, type of account, tax rate, and automatic billing amount.

With *Peachpak 4* accounts receivable, automatic billing is optional for each customer. When you set up your customer files, you can specify that a customer be billed a set amount monthly. Then when you are entering transactions, you can trigger the automatic billing by responding to only one prompt during posting, instead of completing an entire transaction. If you enter a sales tax rate for a customer, the program automatically calculates the taxes when you are entering sales or producing invoices.

Peachpak 4 also features optional consolidation of transactions to save disk storage space. At the end of a financial period, you can consolidate all transactions with the same invoice number, thereby eliminating duplicated or unnecessary detail in records and reports.

Any one of three types of accounts can be assigned to a customer. A regular, or open item, account carries details of open transactions from one accounting period to the next. A balance forward account omits the details and carries forward only a balance due. The third type of account is automatic billing, described previously. For regular accounts, *Peachpak 4* has an open credit reconciliation program that can apply overpayments or prepayments to a particular invoice or consolidate all open credits into one transaction. Open credit reconciliation can be applied to customers or invoices.

You can enter up to nine specific types of transactions into accounts receivable, as well as miscellaneous debits and credits. Specific transaction categories include sales, taxes, freight charge, service charge, payment, credit, adjustment, return, and discount. You can enter a sales transaction without automatically triggering the creation of an invoice.

If you generate an invoice, it will include information on quantity ordered and shipped, unit price, line extensions, freight and service charges, tax, terms of payment, and deposits (see Figure 13.3). Customer statements provide a comprehensive printout of a customer's activity during the period, including the total balance due on the statement date.

To help control cash flow, *Peachpak 4* produces an aged receivables report listing customers and the time outstanding on transactions in accounts receivable. With this report, you will know who should get those automatic dunning messages.

```
* * * * * * * * * * * * * * * * * *
* * *                         * * *
* * *       INVOICE           * * *
* * *                         * * *
* * * * * * * * * * * * * * * * * *
```

ACCOUNT NUMBER: SMITH

INVOICE NO : 2333
INVOICE DATE : 08/18/84
PAGE : 1

SOLD TO	SMITH MFG. 15 CLARK RD. TOLEDO, OH 43614		SHIP TO	SMITH MFG. 15 CLARK RD. TOLEDO, OH 43614

SHIP VIA	: EXEC	YOUR ORDER NO	: 98938393
DELIVERY	: COD	OUR ORDER NO	: PO 35-383-3
SHIP DATE	: 08/19/84	ORDER DATE	: 07/29/84
DUE DATE	: 09/15/84	SALESPERSON	: ABBOTT
TERMS	: 2-10 NET 30		

ITEM	ORD	SHP	DESCRIPTION	PRICE	AMOUNT
34-4328383	24	24	WIDGETS	0.54	12.96
34-3892925	48	48	BOLTS	0.39	18.72
56-383	1	1	MACHINE HOUSING	25.75	25.75
				SUBTOTAL:	57.43

FREIGHT	TAX	SERV O-	MISC DB	DEPOSIT	DISCOUNT	TOTAL
4.89	3.73	0.00	0.00	0.00	5.74	60.31

Figure 13.3 *A sample invoice produced with* Peachpak 4.

Peachpak 4 also produces several other reports for internal use, including a transaction report, a customer status report, a customer account report that lists the information in the current customer file, and a reconcile open credits control report that provides an audit trail of the open credits that you might have consolidated.

The capacities of the accounts receivable program are exactly the same as the general ledger's. If you are using accounts receivable with the general ledger, you must assign account numbers to 11 standard fields when you initialize the receivables program. These fields are identical to the types of transactions the program will accept, including freight charges and discounts. During end-of-period processing, accounts receivable will total the dollar amounts for each of these accounts and transfer them automatically to the general ledger.

Accounts payable The flip side of accounts receivable is accounts payable. The *Peachpak 4* accounts payable program precludes parting with your payments precipitously. All alliteration aside, to maintain cash flow, it is important for a business to delay paying its bills as long as possible and still take advantage of all available discounts. The *Peachpak 4* payables program takes the guesswork out of paying your bills with a variety of automated features and comprehensive reports.

Based on the discounts and due dates that you define for each vendor, the program automatically selects specific invoices for payment over others, helping you take advantage of the best mix of discount, timing, and cash availability. It also prints checks and a check register that shows detailed supporting information.

The program produces a forecast of your cash requirements for open vouchers by due dates or discount dates, so that you can know how much cash you will need in the near future. An open voucher report shows all outstanding vouchers, and an aging report tells you the length of time each voucher has been open. Together these three reports can help you decide which vouchers to pay first. You can also inspect or generate a report about your account status with an individual vendor, including information about current and year-to-date balances, and all transactions in the current period.

The accounts payable program lets you enter prepaid invoices, and you can apply credits against a vendor record or to a specific invoice. Recurring invoices can be automatically posted. Each invoice can be distributed among up to eight general ledger expense accounts if you are using payables with the general ledger. Payables will automatically post summary information to the general ledger as well as to general ledger accounts for cash, discounts, and accounts payable.

The capacities of the accounts payable program are more limited than for the other two *Peachpak 4* modules. The program can handle a maximum of about 400 vendors on one disk. With that number of vendors, you might have room for about 300 to 400 transactions on a double-sided disk. Because the number of transactions is limited only by available disk space, the XT or a PC with a hard disk is the best choice for an accounting system such as *Peachpak 4*.

Each *Peachpak 4* program has the same organization and operating characteristics. System functions are selected from a master menu, and on-screen prompts and help messages are liberally provided. The use of menus and logical procedures makes the program easy to use.

Although *Peachpak 4* may not be a bookkeeping powerhouse, it's an excellent program with which a small business can experience the benefits of automated accounting.

BPI Systems

The programs from BPI Systems are for the professional or the small-business owner who wants the benefits of automated accounting on a personal computer. BPI has considerably more automated functions than *Peachpak 4*, and it also has greater data storage and retrieval capacities and includes a payroll program.

Documentation The documentation is excellent and includes detailed references to configuring the system, to setting up the accounting system, and to key functions. Each program has a manual in a three-ring binder that also contains the program disks. There are three disks for the *General Accounting* program: a StartUp disk, which loads the operating system and enables you to perform various DOS functions such as formatting and copying; the Program disk; and the Sample disk, which teaches the program's operation. Other programs have more than one program disk as well as the start-up and sample data disks.

The manuals are well written and well organized. The first parts lead you through various exercises using sample data. The reader is always given step-by-step instructions for using the program, and there are excellent sections on problem solving. Even if you don't know much about accounting, you can follow these manuals easily, although the manufacturer warns that you should be familiar with accounting practices to operate the programs. The tables of contents and indexes are detailed and thorough.

General ledger *General Accounting*—BPI's general ledger program—functions well as a stand-alone system. The program can accommodate up to 2000 accounts, which can be divided among general, payroll, accounts payable, and accounts receivable ledgers, as well as payees and payors. You can set up separate ledgers for employees, vendors, and customers, and keep detailed records of transactions within these three groups. Although these ledgers are not as detailed as those produced by other BPI modules, they are adequate if you are using a general accounting program as a stand-alone system.

For each customer, the *General Accounting* program's accounts receivable ledger reports balance owed, current month's payments on account, and current month's charges. The program automatically posts transactions from the various journals and registers to this ledger, and you can enter transactions for a customer without having to type in a customer's name by typing a C and the customer's identification number.

The accounts payable ledger gives information about vendors, including the balance owed and current payments. Typing a V and the vendor's identification number is a quick way to enter vendor-related transactions.

The payroll ledger report details employees' earnings and deductions monthly, quarterly, or year to date (see Figure 13.4). When you get around to paying all those employees and vendors, *General Accounting* uses data from the cash disbursements journal to write checks automatically.

FAIRVIEW DISTRIBUTING COMPANY
QTD AND YTD PAYROLL LEDGER

AS OF 6/30/83 PAGE 1

EMP NO.	EMPLOYEE NAME	G/L ACCT	CURRENT	QUARTER TO-DATE	YEAR TO-DATE
123	BLANCHARD, E.				
	SALARIES-DEPT. 1	6044	403.85	5,250.00	10,500.00
	FICA PAYABLE	2040	27.06 –	351.75 –	703.50 –
	FEDERAL INCOME TAX W/	2050	26.25 –	341.25 –	682.50 –
	STATE INCOME TAX W/H	2070	8.08 –	105.00 –	210.00 –
	NET PAY		342.46	4,452.00	8,904.00
124	DUFFY, K.				
	SALARIES-DEPT. 1	6044	.00	2,450.00	4,900.00
	FICA PAYABLE	2040	.00	164.15 –	328.30 –
	FEDERAL INCOME TAX W/	2050	.00	159.25 –	318.50 –
	STATE INCOME TAX W/H	2070	.00	49.00 –	98.00 –
	NET PAY		.00	2,077.60	4,155.20
125	SMITH, G.F.				
	SALARIES-DEPT. 1	6044	326.92	4,250.00	8,500.00
	FICA PAYABLE	2040	21.90 –	284.75 –	569.50 –
	FEDERAL INCOME TAX W/	2050	21.25 –	276.25 –	552.50 –
	STATE INCOME TAX W/H	2070	6.54 –	85.00 –	170.00 –
	NET PAY		277.23	3,304.00	7,208.00
SUMMARIES					
	SALARIES-DEPT. 1	6044	730.77	11,950.00	23,900.00
	FICA PAYABLE	2040	48.96 –	800.65 –	1,601.30 –
	FEDERAL INCOME TAX W/	2050	47.50 –	776.75 –	1,553.50 –
	STATE INCOME TAX W/H	2070	14.62 –	239.00 –	478.00 –
	NET PAY		619.69	10,133.60	20,267.20

Figure 13.4 *A sample payroll ledger produced with BPI Systems'* General Accounting *module.*

BPI Systems offers efficient ways to enter transactions. You'll remember that most transactions with *Peachpak 4* had to be in double-entry form. With BPI you simply enter the transaction, and the program automatically records it as a double-entry, either to control accounts that you have defined or to subsidiary ledgers. Regular monthly entries, such as depreciation, can be consolidated and made at the end of each month with one command. You can also enter data files from external sources either manually into the general journal each month, or automatically into the program.

The manuals explain that you have to know a little about computer programming to prepare the data for automatic merging, and you should heed that warning, because you could seriously damage the entire accounting system by dumping in a bad file. The user manual includes an appendix to help you create external files having the proper format, and emphasizes that you don't have to use this feature if you don't want to.

BPI's *General Accounting* produces the standard trial balance, balance sheet, and income statement reports. You can have consolidated income statements or statements for up to ten departments or divisions. The program also generates summaries of the activity in ledgers and journals, and schedules of accounts, customers, vendors, employees, and payee/payors. The reports don't have many frills, but they contain the necessary basic information.

BPI offers two basic security features for those who need to safeguard accounting data from unauthorized users. You can require the use of a six-character code for your company and, for extra security, a six-character password that will not appear on the screen when entered. System users won't be able to enter data into the system without entering the company code and the password.

Accounts receivable BPI's *Accounts Receivable* program features the same flexibility and ease of data entry as the general accounting module. Accounts receivable can be based on either the balance forward or the open item method. There are four types of customer accounts that you can maintain: the normal accounts receivable account; a repetitive charge account, which is a normal account that can also accept periodic fixed charges; a revolving charge account, which requires a minimum payment each period; and a fixed payment account, which requires the customer to pay a fixed installment each month on the unpaid balance.

The program automatically does double-entry accounting, just as the *General Accounting* program does. If you are using the open item accounting method, each invoice on a customer's account stays open until payment is specifically credited to that account. With BPI, you can apply a customer's payment to an individual invoice or, by issuing one command, to all the open invoices. You can also age all the accounts by one billing period and ready the program for the next period's activity with just one command.

BPI enables you to set two levels of finance charges, as well as the minimum balance that finance charges will be applied to. For instance, you might decide to levy a charge of 6 percent against balances from $50 to $100, and 5 percent for balances above $100.

Accounts Receivable produces an excellent range of reports and other materials. For example, the program not only produces statements for all customers, active customers only, selected customers only, or customers having past due balances, but also prints mailing labels. You can enter two special message lines of up to 50 characters each at the bottom of each statement, as well as the payment due date. Reports are available that can analyze the accounts receivable status of all accounts, selective accounts, current or year-to-date past due accounts, and accounts for which finance charges have been waived.

The *Accounts Receivable* program has excellent capacities, especially if you are using an XT. With a two-floppy-disk-drive system, you can have up to 1000 separate customer accounts, and with the XT or another fixed disk system, 2000 customers. Each customer account can accommodate up to 360 transactions per billing period. The *Accounts Receivable* general ledger itself can hold up to 120 accounts.

Accounts payable You can use either accrual or cash basis accounting with BPI's *Accounts Payable* program, and if you're using the accrual method, you can have two fiscal periods open at the same time to help keep the accounts in balance. If you have two periods open at once, the payables check register records check information for either period.

The program automatically writes checks, either for individual vouchers, to individual vendors, or for all open vouchers on a selected due date. Even though the check-writing process is automated, a specific command enables you to select and review the checks you want to print and change them if necessary before printing.

Like the other BPI Systems modules, *Accounts Payable* features automatic double-entry transaction entry. You can also speed up data entry by using the program's "prompts" feature. To use the prompts feature, you set up the program to distribute transactions to "usual" accounts. When you are ready, the program prompts you with the usual account's name, and you press <Enter> to enter the transaction.

The payables module has all the reports you need to monitor your payments due and choose the best mix of bills to settle. A cash requirements report shows how much cash you will need to meet obligations up to a selected date, and various reports on aged payables help you make your payments on time. The program also prints mailing labels.

The capacities of *Accounts Payable* are somewhat smaller than those of *Accounts Receivable*. For any one company, the program can hold up to 550 general ledger accounts, 450 regular vendors, and 200 casual vendors. You can draw on up to 10 checking accounts, and credit up to 14 vouchers on a check stub. The maximum number of vouchers is 1000 per accounting period, with 200 vouchers per check run. Although you can use *Accounts Payable* with *General Accounting*, there are two other BPI programs that are designed to work automatically with payables: job cost and inventory control.

Payroll The BPI Systems *Payroll* program can transfer data automatically to the other BPI programs, and it has some very powerful features. It has the BPI automatic double-entry and can write checks automatically at the end of each pay period and produce W-2 forms at the end of the year. If you want to write checks and W-2s manually, you can. When your employees go on vacation, the program can issue a single check that covers both regular pay and a vacation advance, but it will account for the taxes and deductions on the vacation pay as though two checks had been issued.

This package can pay employees in three ways: by salary, hourly, and on commission. Commissions can be figured in four ways, and if you're paying hourly, up to three rates for each employee can be specified.

The BPI *Payroll* module is especially efficient at withholding taxes, even down to the district level. It can calculate federal and state tax withholding for all 50 states. It can withhold city and county taxes for both residents and nonresidents of Maryland and New York City, and for residents of Michigan cities and Indiana counties. It can even hold back State Disability Insurance taxes for Californians. The program can withhold taxes for Puerto Rico, the District of Columbia, New Jersey, and New York.

If your company has an employer-sponsored individual retirement account, BPI's *Payroll* can keep track of employees' contributions. To the delight of the IRS, it will also keep track of their tips. You can specify up to 20 optional deductions, and any 6 may be assigned to any one employee. Three automatic deductions—FICA, federal tax, and state tax—are included for each employee, for a total of 9 deductions per employee. *Payroll* can maintain up to 150 payroll general ledger accounts, with up to 230 employees on one disk (if you're using doubled-sided disk drives and disks). With the XT or a similar hard disk, you can have up to 6000 employees on one disk. For every pay period, you can make up to 250 entries to the general journal. With these capacities, you can run a payroll for a substantial business.

All four BPI Systems accounting programs running together make a formidable accounting system for any small or medium-sized business. In addition to the outstanding features of each program, all the BPI programs operate equally well. The menus and prompts are easy to follow and use, and the tutorial disks and exercises that are a part of each program help you learn quickly.

The user manual for each program has detailed instructions for setting up the automatic interface with other BPI programs. The manual includes an exercise on interfacing using the sample data disks, and checklists help to ensure that you follow all the right steps when you make the connection with real data.

BPI Systems programs have sophisticated features, excellent documentation, and ease of use. Used with the IBM PC or XT, they make up a fine accounting system.

CHAPTER FOURTEEN

Specialized Applications Software

Many valuable specialized business applications for the PC and the XT don't fit into the major categories of applications discussed so far. Some programs deal with "vertical market" applications; they work for only one type of business, such as real estate management, construction, or the legal profession. Other vertical markets include medical applications, engineering, and telemarketing. Because of their narrowly defined markets, these profession-specific programs are not discussed here.

A number of other specialized programs are not limited to particular occupations. These programs include software for investment analysis, project management, and time management. Another specialized program has established a new software category; the program is *TK!Solver* (Software Arts), and the category is equation processing. Still other specialized programs enhance word processing, by both managing and analyzing text.

One final category of specialized software has the potential for use with every PC: communications software, which controls computer-to-computer data transfer. With a modem and the proper communications program, you can exchange information with other personal computers and with much larger computers that contain vast data bases.

Investment Analysis

Investment analysis software is a great improvement over its manual alternative. An investment analysis program processes the data that many investors use to buy and manage stocks. For example, these programs provide such functions as studying and charting historical price and volume data for individual stocks, and attempting to predict the future action of a stock based on that history.

One of the best investment analysis programs for the PC is the *Dow Jones Market Analyzer* (Dow Jones & Co.), which was designed to work with information from the Dow Jones News/Retrieval financial data base, probably the best source for that kind of information. The program accesses information from the Dow Jones News/Retrieval service and then uses that data to produce charts on a stock's price and volume history. As befits technical analysis, the output is sophisticated. To get the most out of the program, you have to understand the technical approach to the stock market.

Project Management

What spreadsheets have done for financial analysis models, project schedulers have done for managing large, complex projects. These programs are structured to assist with two major areas of project management: planning and control. You enter the major variables of a project, such as starting and ending dates, tasks to be performed, and costs, and the program schedules the fastest, most cost-effective way to complete the job.

Like a spreadsheet, project schedulers have a "what if" capability. You can test the results of changes in completion dates, costs, number of tasks, and other variables, and the program automatically shows you the results of the variations. What if the inevitable happens, and delays or changes of plans plague a project? The program can forecast the effects of those changes on the rest of the job.

Some project management programs can plot the critical path of a project, or the sequence of tasks that will yield the optimum efficiency in completing the project. Critical path scheduling helps you concentrate on the parts of the project that are most important and avoid wasting resources on nonessential tasks. The better project management programs can calculate the critical path and recalculate it when scheduling changes occur.

One of the first project management programs for personal computers, and still one of the most popular, is *Visi-Schedule* (VisiCorp), which can handle up to 160 tasks per project, with up to nine prerequisites per task. It can calculate up to nine skill categories assigned to a project and their costs per task; manpower levels and manpower costs; and start, end, and deadline dates for each task. This type of program is especially useful for planning complex jobs, such as construction of an office building or installation of a large printing press.

The program automatically allocates costs to each task and adjusts the project schedule to level the resources. Detailed reports can be produced for the entire project or any part of it. If any one task in the project slips ahead or behind, the schedule of succeeding tasks is adjusted. If you have ever managed a large construction project, an extended consulting engagement, or a similar, complex job, you will appreciate both the power and the utility of the project management application.

Time Management

Time management programs are like computerized calendars. They manage time and personal information in a convenient, flexible way. But you may not need one of these programs if your schedule is relatively uncomplicated and doesn't change often. In the time it takes to turn on the computer, load DOS, load the program, and make an entry, you can probably make five entries in a conventional calendar.

But if you juggle daily meetings and have to retrieve information quickly for those meetings, this application can be very useful. For a salesperson who makes many calls every day and needs key information about each prospect readily available, a time management program can be a great time saver. *Calendar Management* (Peachtree Software) is a good example of a time management program.

The most basic function of the time manager is keeping your schedule—it alerts you to important upcoming events. The second major function is information storage and retrieval. You can store memos, notes, names, addresses, phone numbers—any information that you need to access quickly. The program usually makes it easy to find information when you need it, because you can use several different keys to file and retrieve the data.

A time management program is useful for people who maintain multiple calendars or arrange meetings for several busy people. And the more electronically integrated your business is, the more effective this kind of program will be. For example, if all the managers in your section were on the same local area network, and their schedules were kept with a time management program, arranging emergency meetings on short notice would be relatively easy. Your individual circumstances will determine whether you need a time management program.

Equation Processors

One application for the PC that is not yet widespread but that promises to be very popular is equation processing. The pioneer program in equation processing is *TK!Solver* (Software Arts). An equation processor solves equations for unknown variables. You supply the equations and the values for the known variables, and the program gives you the correct value for unknown variables. If the program cannot solve an equation, it will tell you why, as well as what it would need to generate a solution. There are many practical applications for equation processing, especially in engineering, science, research, and finance.

TK!Solver is not especially easy to operate. Most people have probably never used anything like it before. And unless you're comfortable with algebraic equations and use them daily in your work, developing a facility for constructing equations might take some time. The program is command-driven and doesn't employ easy-to-learn menus. The commands are not depicted as full words on the screen; they are shown as "slash" commands of single letters, similar to the method used in the original version of *VisiCalc,* which wasn't any easier.

In addition to solving equations for single variables, the program can construct tables of solutions to a single equation. You can use the tables to test various assumptions with different values. A simple example of such a table is the conversion of units of measurement, such as quarts to liters or francs to dollars. *TK!Solver* has a basic graphics capability and can illustrate data produced in tabular form.

To further illustrate the table feature, suppose that you had two equations, one that described the Federal Reserve Bank's M1 money supply and another that calculated the interest rate for 90-day Treasury Bills, using the M1 figure as one of its variables. You could then solve for the T-Bill rate using a wide range of M1 values, and generate a table representing the solutions. *TK!Solver* could then prepare a graph showing the linear relationship of interest rates to money supply, a handy thing to know if you are a portfolio manager trying to invest money in the wisest place.

TK!Solver is structured as a series of "sheets," or data screens. The two primary working sheets are the variable and rule sheets. On the rule sheet, you enter equations and information about variables on the variable sheet, including units of measurement, comments, and input values. There are various subsheets for entering more detailed information about variables. The unit sheet, for example, lets you establish conversion factors, and the variable subsheet lets you differentiate between the units used to solve the equations and the units actually displayed. There are also plot sheets, list sheets, and table sheets. Once you have finished defining your equations, you can press the ! key (the "action" key), and the equations will be solved.

TK!Solver can be used in all phases of business and industry. Those uses might not be obvious at first, however. You need to live with this kind of application for a while to appreciate how much it can do and how useful it can be.

Word Processing Enhancement

Spelling checker, thesaurus, and footnote programs are some of the many applications that extend or enhance word processing programs. Another type of text-oriented program is an idea processor, which generates outlines and helps a writer organize ideas.

Spelling checkers Spelling checkers are helpful, but they are far from perfect; after using one, you may still need to proof text for style, grammar, and typographical errors. If you spell and type fairly well, you might just skip using a spelling checker.

A spelling checker contains a dictionary and compares the words in your text with the entries in the dictionary to find mismatches. When the program finds a mismatch, it marks the word as a possible misspelling. Mismatches are not always misspellings, however; they can also be words that aren't in the program's dictionary.

Spelling checkers mark possible misspellings, but you have to decide whether the word is spelled correctly or not. If it is correct, you have two options. You can add the word to the program's dictionary, so that the program will know the word the next time and avoid flagging it. Most spelling checkers also have a command that makes the program ignore the word and move on if it is correctly spelled, but you don't want to add that particular word to the dictionary. You probably wouldn't want to add proper nouns to a dictionary, for example, even though they may be marked as mismatches.

If a word is misspelled, you would mark it with a special symbol and then use the word processor's search and replace function to find each misspelled word and correct it. One of the newest and best spelling checkers, *VisiSpell* (VisiCorp), enables you to correct misspelled words directly from the *VisiSpell* program—you don't have to leave the spelling checker and load the word processing program. The *Random House ProofReader* (Wang Electronic Publishing, Inc.) has the same feature, as does *The Word Plus* (Oasis Systems).

Some programs help you correct misspelled words. *VisiSpell* displays a suggested correct spelling for the word on the screen. The *Random House ProofReader* and *The Word Plus* provide on-screen dictionaries that prompt you with alternatives. With some programs, however, you're on your own when it comes to making corrections.

Some programs have sophisticated capabilities. *VisiSpell,* for example, can flag double words, such as "for for," and incorrect capitalization, such as "TOday." Other programs enable you to construct special dictionaries by combining existing dictionaries or creating new ones.

The size of the basic dictionary in spelling checker programs varies widely. Because *Super SpellGuard* (Sorcim/IUS Micro Software) has a basic dictionary of 20,200 words, the program can proof text very quickly. But because you will have to stop often to check words that don't match those in the program's dictionary, the speed advantage may be offset. *VisiSpell* has a basic dictionary of 100,000 words, and *ProofReader* comes in three versions: 32,000, 50,000, and 80,000 words. *EasySpeller* (Sorcim/IUS Micro Software) has a dictionary of 88,710 words but is rather slow during execution.

Although most spelling checkers work with several word processing programs, make sure that the program you choose is supported by the word processing program you are using or intend to use. For example, *EasySpeller* will not work with *WordStar,* and *VisiSpell* only works with *VisiWord* (VisiCorp). All the programs accept plain ASCII files.

Thesaurus Using a thesaurus program is another way to augment your word processing program. The *Random House Electronic Thesaurus* (Peachtree Software) offers over 25,000 synonyms, although it is only available as part of *PeachText 5000,* Peachtree's integrated business system, which also includes word processing, a spelling checker, a list manager, and a spreadsheet.

The *Thesaurus* and the word processor are put on the same disk. You can use the *Thesaurus* and still use all the functions of the word processing program. In order to have the program find a synonym, you put the cursor on the first letter of a word, press a function key, and wait to see what the program displays on the screen. If you like the suggested synonym, you can enter it immediately into the text. If no synonym can be found, the program will list the entries from its dictionary immediately before and after the point where the target word would have fit alphabetically.

The program has several shortcomings, however. Like spelling checkers, it is literal and therefore cannot recognize the past tense or plural of words. If you want a synonym for *took,* for example, you won't get any entries for *take.* There are ways to get around this once you understand the problem, but the program is cumbersome.

Because writing a thesaurus program requires a tremendous amount of code, the XT is a perfect vehicle for an expanded version, and one or more are due out soon. Despite all its faults, the *Thesaurus* is an excellent tool for writing, and the upcoming expanded programs should satisfy writers.

Footnoting Another element of word processing, the footnote program, adds to a word processing program what most do not already have: the ability to create footnotes in text in a relatively efficient manner.

One such program, *Footnote* (Digital Marketing), works in conjunction with *WordStar.* After you have produced text with *WordStar,* you switch to *Footnote* and create a file of footnotes. Then you use *Footnote* to merge the files and insert the footnotes in their proper places in the *WordStar* text. Although you can enter footnotes as you are creating text, the process is more difficult than merging files with *Footnote.*

Idea processors A recent addition to the software that concentrates primarily on text is an outlining program, which is also often an idea processor. The original idea processor for the PC is *ThinkTank* (Living Videotext), and that program's popularity prompted Ashton-Tate to add an outlining module to its *Framework* integrated software.

ThinkTank is easy to use, and its purpose is obvious on the screen. You begin by entering a word or phrase as the key idea in an outline, and the program automatically indents the next line in the traditional outline format. You can enter any number of second-level headings, or you can indent one or more lines after you have completed one second-level heading.

The program allows a measure of flexibility with the text; you can move individual entries to the left or right, and you can perform simple searches and sorts within your outline. *ThinkTank* rigidly enforces the outline format, however; you cannot indent a line more than one increment beyond the line above it, nor can you move a line any further to the left than a second level heading.

One very useful feature of the program is its ability to hide headings. The primary heading is always displayed, but all subheadings can be displayed or hidden, allowing you to study the major ideas in an outline without the distraction of seeing all the subordinate ideas. With this feature, even in a long, complex outline, all or most of the major headings can be displayed together on the screen without your having to scroll through a long document.

In short, idea processors such as *ThinkTank* are valuable supplements to word processing, and these programs can help you generate ideas as well as organize information.

Communications

The PC is an excellent information processor and a powerful tool for communications. If your system has a modem and an asynchronous communications card, you can exchange data with other computers at distant locations via the telephone lines. A PC in a branch office, for example, can exchange data with the mainframe computer located at company headquarters. Communications can also be used for electronic mail. Another popular use for communications software is connecting with one of the commercial information services, such as The Source or CompuServe. In addition to these general-interest data bases, there are specialized data bases, such as the Dialog Information Service, that supply information on such diverse topics as medicine, stocks, and the law.

Communications programs can be technically intimidating for first-time users. The jargon associated with modems and communications programs is initially complex. And, unfortunately, you need to understand more than a little of the jargon to make an informed choice of a communications program.

In general, the needs of business users will likely be more complex than those of personal users, because businesses tend to generate heavy communications traffic and need a greater variety of computers connected. But all communications programs have the same core of features that must be present if the software is to be useful.

One important consideration of communications is the speed at which the program sends information over the phone lines. Transfer speed is expressed in baud or bits per second, and the most common rates are 300 and 1200 baud. The most versatile programs can send data at both rates. Another basic feature is the duplex mode. Full-duplex mode enables users to send and receive data simultaneously, while half-duplex mode offers only one-way communication. The program you choose should offer both modes.

A communications program should be able to receive data and immediately store it on disk or keep it in memory for later storage. The better programs can store telephone numbers and even dial automatically (if the modem is capable). You will want a program that supports both manual and automatic dialing. Business users may need a feature called XON/XOFF protocol, which enables you to communicate with some mainframe computers.

One desirable feature is the capability of storing frequently used communications parameters, so that you don't have to go through a lengthy setup procedure every time you want to telecommunicate with another host system. Look for a program that takes full advantage of the function keys, because the program will be easier to use.

One of the most popular communications programs for the PC is *Smartcom II* (Hayes Microcomputer Products). *Smartcom II* is designed to work with the most popular modems for the PC, the Smartmodem series from Hayes. This menu-driven program implements basic features well and has a wide range of advanced features. *Smartcom II* makes good use of macros, automated sequences of instructions that can be stored in the program and invoked with just a few keystrokes. Because *Smartcom II* is menu-driven, it is relatively easy to use, and the program comes with an excellent manual.

Crosstalk XVI (Microstuf) is another communications program with features that are especially useful in a business environment. One of the few features that it does not implement well, however, is the auto-dial directory. This type of directory usually lists and stores phone numbers that an auto-dial modem can access. With *Crosstalk XVI,* the directory lists the file names for the numbers but keeps the numbers in a separate file that can only be accessed with an additional command. The auto-dial feature is not as easy to use as it could be. Despite this minor complaint, however, *Crosstalk XVI* is one of the better communications programs available for the PC.

PC-Talk III (Freeware/The Headlands Press) is an excellent communications program for the PC that is widely available in the public domain. Under the "freeware" plan developed by Andrew Fluegelman, creator of *PC-Talk III,* anyone who wants a copy of the program is encouraged, but not required, to send a $35 donation. *PC-Talk*'s third version would be a bargain at a much higher price, because it is a full-featured program. *PC-Talk III* also has a feature called the Xmodem protocol, a file transfer protocol that helps ensure error-free data transmission. You will have to print the documentation, however, because it comes only on disk.

Personal computers are excellent tools for enhancing personal productivity, but they are at least as effective when they connect people and information sources. Communications software can literally put libraries of information at your fingertips. It is well worth the investment and the time it takes to learn to use these programs.

The List Goes On

There are still other applications for the PC that you may find interesting: programs that help compute taxes, manage property, run medical offices, and so on. If you want to find out more about some of these applications, read some of the PC-specific magazines, such as *PC World* and *Softalk for the IBM PC.* Other magazines review business software exclusively, and many if not most of the programs reviewed will be available for the PC and the XT. Computer dealers and user groups may also be helpful.

Given the runaway popularity of the PC and the XT, you can be sure that exciting innovations in software will always be available for your computer.

Appendix: Products and Manufacturers

Following are products mentioned in this book. The software requirements represent the minimum needed to run each program; the amount of memory needed assumes DOS 2.00 or higher.

Software

Accounts Payable,
Accounts Receivable,
General Accounting, Payroll
BPI Systems, Inc.
3423 Guadalupe
Austin, TX 78705
512/454-2801
Requirements: 128K, two floppy disk drives or one floppy disk drive and a hard disk

BPS Business Graphics
Business & Professional Software
143 Binney St.
Cambridge, MA 02142
617/491-3377, 800/DIALBPS
Requirements: 128K, at least two floppy disk drives, IBM Color/Graphics Adapter

Business Graphics System
Peachtree Software, Inc.
3445 Peachtree Rd.
Atlanta, GA 30326
404/239-3000
Requirements: 128K, two disk drives

CalcStar
MicroPro International Corporation
33 San Pablo Ave.
San Rafael, CA 94903
415/499-1200, 800/443-0100 x948
(dealer referral)
Requirements: 128K, two disk drives

Calendar Management
Peachtree Software, Inc.
3445 Peachtree Rd.
Atlanta, GA 30326
404/239-3000
Requirements: 128K, two disk drives

Crosstalk XVI
Microstuf, Inc.
1000 Holcomb Woods Pkwy. #440
Roswell, GA 30076
404/998-3998
Requirements: 96K, one disk drive, asynchronous communications adapter

Data Base Manager II–The Integrator
Alpha Software Corporation
30 B St.
Burlington, MA 01803
617/229-2924, 800/451-1018, 800/462-2016 in Massachusetts
Requirements: 128K, two disk drives

dBASE II
Ashton-Tate
10150 W. Jefferson Blvd.
Culver City, CA 90230
213/204-5570
Requirements: 128K, one disk drive

dBASE III
Ashton-Tate
10150 W. Jefferson Blvd.
Culver City, CA 90230
213/204-5570
Requirements: 256K, two floppy disk drives or one floppy disk drive and a hard disk

DesQ
Quarterdeck Office Systems
1918 Main St.
Santa Monica, CA 90405
800/845-6621, 213/392-9852
Requirements: 320K (512K recommended), 5M hard disk; mouse optional

dGRAPH
Fox & Geller, Inc.
604 Market St.
Elmwood Park, NJ 07407
201/794-8883
Requirements: 128K, one disk drive, graphics monitor and color graphics board for color

Dow Jones Market Analyzer
Dow Jones & Co., Inc.
P.O. Box 300
Princeton, NJ 08540
609/452-2000, 800/257-5114, 609/452-1511 in New Jersey, Alaska, and Hawaii
Requirements: 128K, one disk drive, asynchronous communications adapter with RS-232-compatible modem, special printer to support graphics

EasySpeller
Sorcim/IUS Micro Software
2401 Marinship Way
Sausalito, CA 94965
415/331-6700
Requirements: 128K, two disk drives

Extended Report Writer
Microrim, Inc.
3380 146th Pl. SE
Bellevue, WA 98007
206/641-6619
Requirements: 256K, two disk drives

Footnote
Digital Marketing Corporation
2363 Boulevard Circle #8
Walnut Creek, CA 94595
415/947-1000, 800/826-2222
Requirements: 128K, one disk drive, *WordStar* or *Select* word processing program

Framework
Ashton-Tate
10150 W. Jefferson Blvd.
Culver City, CA 90230
213/204-5570
Requirements: 256K, two disk drives

Friday!
Ashton-Tate
10150 W. Jefferson Blvd.
Culver City, CA 90230
213/204-5570
Requirements: 128K, two floppy disk drives or one floppy disk drive and a hard disk

MBA
Context Management Systems
23868 Hawthorne Blvd.
Torrance, CA 90505
213/378-8277
Requirements: 256K, two disk drives, IBM Color/Graphics Adapter

Microsoft Windows
Microsoft Corporation
10700 Northup Way
Bellevue, WA 98004
206/828-8080
Requirements: 192K, two disk drives, pointing device

Microsoft Word
Microsoft Corporation
10700 Northup Way
Bellevue, WA 98004
206/828-8080
Requirements: 128K, one disk drive

MultiMate
MultiMate International
52 Oakland Ave. N
East Hartford, CT 06108
203/522-2116
Requirements: 256K, two disk drives

Multiplan
Microsoft Corporation
10700 Northup Way
Bellevue, WA 98004
206/828-8080
Requirements: 128K, one disk drive

Multiplan Applications: ***Budget*** and ***Financial Statement***
Microsoft Corporation
10700 Northup Way
Bellevue, WA 98004
206/828-8080
Requirements: 128K, one disk drive

1-2-3
Lotus Development Corporation
161 First St.
Cambridge, MA 02142
617/492-7171, 617/253-9150 (product support and customer service)
Requirements: 192K, two disk drives, color graphics board or dot matrix printer for graphics component

Open Access
Software Products International
10240 Sorrento Valley Rd.
San Diego, CA 92121
619/450-1526
Requirements: 192K, two floppy disk drives or one floppy disk drive and a hard disk, graphics and communications supporting hardware optional

Peachpak 4
Peachtree Software, Inc.
3445 Peachtree Rd.
Atlanta, GA 30326
404/239-3000
Requirements: 64K, two disk drives

PeachText 5000
Peachtree Software, Inc.
3445 Peachtree Rd.
Atlanta, GA 30326
404/239-3000
Requirements: 128K, two disk drives

PC-Talk III
Freeware/The Headlands Press, Inc.
P.O. Box 862
Tiburon, CA 94920
Requirements: 64K (128K for compiled version), one disk drive

PeachText Word Processor with the ***Random House Electronic Thesaurus***
Peachtree Software, Inc.
3445 Peachtree Rd.
Atlanta, GA 30326
404/239-3000
Requirements: 96K, two disk drives

pfs:file, pfs:report
Software Publishing Corporation
1901 Landings Dr.
Mountain View, CA 94043
415/962-8910
Requirements: 64K, one disk drive

pfs:graph
Software Publishing Corporation
1901 Landings Dr.
Mountain View, CA 94043
415/962-8910
Requirements: 128K, one disk drive

Quickcode
Fox & Geller, Inc.
604 Market St.
Elmwood Park, NJ 07407
201/794-8883
Requirements: 180K, two disk drives or one floppy disk drive and a hard disk

Random House ProofReader
Wang Electronic Publishing, Inc.
1 Industrial Ave.
Lowell, MA 01851
617/967-4541
Requirements: 64K with one floppy disk drive, 128K with one floppy disk drive and a hard disk

R:base 4000
Microrim, Inc.
3380 146th Pl. SE
Bellevue, WA 98007
206/641-6619
Requirements: 256K, two disk drives

Smartcom II
Hayes Microcomputer Products, Inc.
5923 Peachtree Industrial Blvd.
Norcross, GA 30092
404/449-8791
Requirements: 96K, one disk drive, Smartmodem 300, 1200, or 1200B

StarBurst
MicroPro International Corporation
33 San Pablo Ave.
San Rafael, CA 94903
415/499-1200
Requirements: 96K, two disk drives (hard disk recommended)

SuperCalc
Sorcim/IUS Micro Software
2195 Fortune Dr.
San Jose, CA 95131
408/942-1727
Requirements: 64K, one disk drive

SuperCalc3
Sorcim/IUS Micro Software
2195 Fortune Dr.
San Jose, CA 95131
408/942-1727
Requirements: 96K, two disk drives

Super SpellGuard
Sorcim/IUS Micro Software
2195 Fortune Dr.
San Jose, CA 95131
408/942-1727
Requirements: 32K, one disk drive

Symphony
Lotus Development Corporation
161 First St.
Cambridge, MA 02142
617/492-7171
Requirements: 320K, one disk drive

The Word Plus
Oasis Systems
7907 Ostrow St., Ste. F
San Diego, CA 92111
619/279-5711
Requirements: 128K, one disk drive (two are recommended)

ThinkTank
Living Videotext, Inc.
2432 Charleston Rd.
Mountain View, CA 94043
415/964-6300
Requirements: 256K, two disk drives

TK!Solver
Software Arts
27 Mica Ln.
Wellesley, MA 02181
617/237-4000
Requirements: 96K, one disk drive

VisiCalc
VisiCorp
2895 Zanker Rd.
San Jose, CA 95134
408/946-9000, 408/942-6000 (customer support)
Requirements: 64K, one disk drive

VisiCalc Advanced Version
Software Arts
27 Mica Ln.
Wellesley, MA 02181
617/237-4000
Requirements: 196K, two disk drives

Visi On Applications Manager, Visi On Calc, Visi On Graph, Visi On Word
VisiCorp
2895 Zanker Rd.
San Jose, CA 95134
408/946-9000, 408/942-6000 (customer support)
Requirements: 512K, one floppy disk drive, one hard disk, graphics board and graphics monitor to run windows

VisiSchedule
VisiCorp
2895 Zanker Rd.
San Jose, CA 95134
408/946-9000, 408/942-6000 (customer support)
Requirements: 64K, two disk drives

VisiSpell
VisiCorp
2895 Zanker Rd.
San Jose, CA 95134
408/946-9000, 408/942-6000 (customer support)
Requirements: 128K, two disk drives

VisiTrend/Plot
VisiCorp
2895 Zanker Rd.
San Jose, CA 95134
408/946-9000, 408/942-6000 (customer support)
Requirements: 192K, color graphics board, high resolution graphics monitor, special printer to support graphics

VisiWord (also sold as *VisiWord Plus,* which includes *VisiSpell*)
VisiCorp
2895 Zanker Rd.
San Jose, CA 95134
408/946-9000, 408/942-6000 (customer support)
Requirements: 192K, two disk drives

Volkswriter Executive
Lifetree Software, Inc.
411 Pacific St. #315
Monterey, CA 93940
408/373-4718
Requirements: 64K, one disk drive

WordStar Professional (***WordStar, CorrectStar, MailMerge,*** and ***StarIndex*** may also be purchased separately)
MicroPro International Corporation
33 San Pablo Ave.
San Rafael, CA 94903
415/499-1200, 800/443-0100 x948
Requirements: 64K, one disk drive

Hardware

Compaq computer
Compaq Computer Corporation
20333 FM 149
Houston, TX 77070
713/370-7040

Columbia computer
Columbia Data Products, Inc.
9150D Rumsey Rd.
Columbia, MD 21045
301/992-3400

Eagle computer
Eagle Computer, Inc.
983 University Ave.
Los Gatos, CA 95030
408/395-5005

Epson dot matrix printers
Epson America, Inc.
3415 Kashiwa St.
Torrance, CA 90505
800/421-5426, 213/539-9140 in California

Hercules Graphics Card
Hercules Computer Technology
2550 Ninth St. #210
Berkeley, CA 94710
415/540-6000

Hiplot plotters
Houston Instruments
8500 Cameron Rd.
Austin, TX 78753
800/531-5479

HP plotters
Hewlett-Packard
16399 W. Bernardo Dr.
San Diego, CA 92127
619/487-4100, 800/367-4722

IBM dot matrix printers
IBM
Systems Products Division
P.O. Box 1328
Boca Raton, FL 33432
800/447-4700, 800/322-4400 in Illinois, 800/447-0890 in Alaska and Hawaii

PC Mouse
Mouse Systems Corporation
2336 H Walsh Ave.
Santa Clara, CA 95051
408/988-0211

TI Professional computer
Texas Instruments Incorporated
P.O. Box 402430
Dallas, TX 75240

Patrick Plemmons has extensive experience in personal computer applications in business. He holds a master's degree in management and is currently a consultant with an international executive search firm. He has also worked as a management consultant with Booz, Allen & Hamilton, a major management consulting firm, and was Vice President for Strategic Planning/Marketing for a multi-hospital system for four years. He is the principal author of Personal Computer Buyer's Guide (VisiPress, 1984).

The following people contributed to this book:

Editor: Jeremy Joan Hewes; *Consulting Editors, PC World:* David Bunnell, Andrew Fluegelman; *Consulting Editor, Simon & Schuster:* Robert C. Eckhardt; *Editorial Production Manager:* Betsy Dilernia; *Editorial staff:* Lindy Wankoff, Evelyn Spire, Joanne Clapp; *Designer:* Marjorie Spiegelman; *Production staff:* Rebecca Oliver, Sharon Smith, Wendy Schwartz; *Typesetter:* Design & Type, San Francisco.

Each of the following products is a trademark or a registered trademark of the company listed in parentheses after the product name.

Software

Accounts Payable, Accounts Receivable, General Accounting, Payroll (BPI Systems, Inc.), *BPS Business Graphics* (Business & Professional Software), *Business Graphics System, Calendar Management, Peachpak 4, PeachText 5000, PeachText Word Processor with the Random House Electronic Thesaurus* (Peachtree, Inc.), *CalcStar, WordStar Professional (WordStar, CorrectStar, MailMerge, StarIndex), StarBurst* (MicroPro International Corporation), *Crosstalk XVI* (Microstuf, Inc.), *Data Base Manager II–The Integrator* (Alpha Software Corporation), *dBASE II, dBASE III, Framework, Friday!* (Ashton-Tate), *DesQ* (Quarterdeck Office Systems), *dGRAPH, Quickcode* (Fox & Geller, Inc.), *Dow Jones Market Analyzer* (Dow Jones & Co., Inc.), *EasySpeller, SuperCalc, SuperCalc3, Super SpellGuard* (Sorcim/IUS Micro Software), *Extended Report Writer, R:base 4000* (Microrim, Inc.), *Footnote* (Digital Marketing Corporation), *MBA* (Context Management Systems), *Budget, Financial Statement, Microsoft Windows, Microsoft Word, Multiplan* (Microsoft Corporation), *MultiMate* (MultiMate International), *1-2-3, Symphony* (Lotus Development Corporation), *Open Access* (Software Products International), *PC-Talk III* (Freeware/The Headlands Press, Inc.), *pfs:file, pfs:graph, pfs:report* (Software Publishing Corporation), *Random House ProofReader* (Wang Electronic Publishing, Inc.), *Smartcom II* (Hayes Microcomputer Products, Inc.), *The Word Plus* (Oasis Systems), *ThinkTank* (Living Videotext, Inc.), *TK!Solver, VisiCalc Advanced Version* (Software Arts), *VisiCalc, Visi On Applications Manager, Visi On Calc, Visi On Graph, Visi On Word, VisiSchedule, VisiSpell, VisiTrend/Plot, VisiWord* (VisiCorp), *Volkswriter Executive* (Lifetree Software, Inc.).

Hardware

Compaq (Compaq Computer Corporation), Columbia (Columbia Data Products, Inc.), Eagle (Eagle Computer, Inc.), Epson (Epson America, Inc.), Hercules Graphics Card (Hercules Computer Technology), HP plotters (Hewlett-Packard), Hiplot plotters (Houston Instruments), IBM (International Business Machines Corporation), PC Mouse (Mouse Systems Corporation), TI Professional (Texas Instruments Incorporated).

Index

Page numbers in italic indicate definitions.

Other PC World Books

Getting Started with the IBM PC and XT

by David Arnold and the Editors of PC World

In *Getting Started with the IBM PC and XT,* David Arnold and the Editors of PC World have teamed up to give PC users a clearly written, authoritative guide to using the PC and its more powerful cousin, the XT. If you are new to the computer, you will value the tutorial approach to becoming familiar with the keyboard, the disks, and the disk operating system (DOS 1.10 and 2.00) and to learning how to set up and handle electronic files. You will appreciate the careful explanations of how to evaluate your software needs and the practical introduction to BASIC, which includes essential commands for file management as well as programming. If you are already working with the PC or the XT and want to explore further, you can count on *Getting Started* for detailed explanations and examples of advanced aspects of DOS 2.00 and special XT requirements, such as hard disk formatting. The book also includes a section on the maintenance and care of electronic equipment. Whether you're just beginning to use a PC or need a handy reference manual, this book will help you master the many facets of your computer and keep it running smoothly.

How to Buy an IBM PC or Compatible Computer

by Danny Goodman and the Editors of PC World

More people buy the IBM PC and PC compatibles than any other personal computers. But the PC and compatibles come in many configurations for many different tasks, and selecting an appropriate system is not always easy. This comprehensive, easy-to-understand guide is exactly what you need to save yourself hours of unnecessary effort and confusion. *How to Buy an IBM PC or Compatible Computer* answers all the common questions that frustrate buyers and also addresses many other issues that are often overlooked, such as matching the system to the work it must perform (including decisions about memory size, type of disk drives, displays and printers, conservation of expansion slots, and choice of essential software), evaluating dealers and salespeople, and selecting a maintenance organization and contract. The authors discuss the complex issue of PC compatibility and describe the most important PC-compatible computers. In today's crowded and confusing computer marketplace, *How to Buy an IBM PC or Compatible Computer* is the perfect guide to making sensible decisions about one of the most important purchases you'll ever make.

Communications for the IBM PC and XT

by Lisa B. Stahr and the Editors of PC World

One of the truly exciting features of personal computers is their ability to exchange information with each other—and with distant mainframe computers—over the telephone lines. *Communications for the IBM PC and XT* provides a window to resources that extend beyond your PC. Clear, comprehensive, and thought-provoking, the book explains how to select the most appropriate communications software and peripherals for your PC and offers a nontechnical look at how computers actually communicate with each other. The authors explain how to use the different types of communications to best suit your professional and personal needs, including conducting research on commercial data bases; acquiring software—sometimes for free—directly over the phone lines; exchanging messages on an electronic bulletin board; and linking several PCs and XTs into a local area network so that you and your group can perform your work more efficiently than ever. No matter what your specific needs are, *Communications for the IBM PC and XT* will help you make the most of your computer's ability to join forces with other computers.

Hardware for the IBM PC and XT

by Frederic E. Davis, Seth Novogrodsky, and the Editors of PC World

Hardware for the IBM PC and XT is an invaluable guide and reference that will help you make sense of the continually expanding and sometimes perplexing array of add-on equipment available for the PC, XT, and PC-compatible computers. If you're a newcomer to the PC, the general introductions to the entire array of peripherals—from such familiar devices as keyboards, game controllers, and monitors to more exotic possibilities such as voice recognition devices, bubble memory, and graphics plotters—will provide the basis for understanding each type of device and its uses. If you already know how you want to expand your system, you can consult the digests of major brand-name products to narrow your choices. Each product listing contains a complete description of the peripheral and its capabilities, as well as a discussion of the important criteria for evaluating features. *Hardware for the IBM PC and XT* opens up new worlds of personal computing by helping you expand your system sensibly, efficiently, and precisely to your needs.

Learning and Having Fun with the IBM PC and PCjr

by Fred D'Ignazio and the Editors of PC World

You may think the IBM PC is all work and no play—not true! *Learning and Having Fun with the IBM PC and PCjr* is a delightful, informative look at the vast array of educational and recreational software available for the IBM PC and PCjr (which is designed for games and learning programs). Fred D'Ignazio and the Editors of PC World look at the main areas of educational and recreational computing—from math and spelling programs to mind-boggling adventures and sophisticated tutorials. They provide the criteria for determining what constitutes a good game or learning program and evaluate the best and most important software available today. The book contains hands-on examples of games and educational programs that will enable you to take advantage of the many features of the PC and PCjr and design your own games. Take a break from your spreadsheets and data bases— don your aviator glasses or strap on Excalibur—and start *Learning and Having Fun with the IBM PC and PCjr.*

The Fully Powered PC

by Burton L. Alperson, Andrew Fluegelman, Lawrence J. Magid, and the Editors of PC World

Now that you own a PC and have been working with it for some time, are you starting to wish it had just a few more special features to help you do your job better? Perhaps a way to execute a command in one keystroke that now takes six? Or a way to make a section of internal memory act like a disk—but fifty times faster? Are you running out of expansion slots, even though you can think of a dozen more boards you'd like to add? Relax—and read *The Fully Powered PC,* the first and only guide devoted exclusively to ways of customizing the highly versatile PC with modestly priced software and hardware additions, including keyboard reconfiguration programs, spoolers, custom-designed menus, batch filers, and multifunction expansion boards (to squeeze even more capabilities into one expansion slot). With up-to-the-minute guidance from the experts, you'll be able to create a computer system exactly as you want it. When you're ready to take full advantage of your computing capabilities, shift into high gear with *The Fully Powered PC.*

Logo for the IBM PC and PCjr

by David Myers and the Editors of PC World

As the personal computer revolution spreads, more and more computer owners have become aware of Logo, which is rapidly emerging as the language of choice for teaching children the fundamentals of computers, programming, and logical thinking. But did you know that Logo is not just for children, and that it's not just a language that makes it easy to create graphics on your computer? *Logo for the IBM PC and PCjr* leads adults and children alike into the world of Logo programming. The book shows you how this elegant, easy-to-learn language can be used to both understand computers and create practical programs that are not available commercially. Using a hands-on, tutorial approach, David Myers and the Editors of PC World take you beyond most other books on Logo, explaining clearly and completely the many fascinating features of this language, including creating turtle graphics, animating sprites, learning how to define your own Logo commands, and even programming your PC or PCjr to converse with you in plain English. And, of course, *Logo for the IBM PC and PCjr* is filled with many sample Logo programs that are both practical and fun.

Hands On: Useful Tips and Routines for the IBM PC and XT

by the Editors of PC World

For everyone who enjoys the vast number of practical tips and useful articles that have appeared in *PC World* since the magazine's first issue, the Editors of PC World have collected the best of the "Hands On" section of the magazine. This book covers both hardware and software, and it is clearly organized so that you can quickly find information on virtually anything you need to know about your PC: instructions for installing boards and disk drives, troubleshooting hardware problems, patching programs to utilize the special features of various printers, and increasing programming efficiency. Additional chapters of the book detail specific program applications, such as creating a checkbook ledger with Lotus *1-2-3,* printing envelopes, labels, and other odd-sized documents with *WordStar,* keeping tax records on *dBASE II,* and tracking investments with *SuperCalc. Hands On* is the definitive collection of "how-to's" for your PC from the experts in the field, the Editors of PC World.

Making the Most of the IBM PCjr

by David Myers and the Editors of PC World

In the same way that the IBM PC has become the dominant force in personal computers, the IBM Home Computer—the PCjr—is emerging as an equally exciting and impressive force among family oriented machines. To introduce you to the PCjr and to computing in general, David Myers and the Editors of PC World have applied their expertise to describing this fascinating machine, providing you and your family with the perfect guide to making the most of the PCjr. *Making the Most of the IBM PCjr* includes detailed and easy-to-understand instructions for using the cordless keyboard, color monitors and television sets for graphics displays, the disk operating system, cartridge and disk-based software, and the most important peripherals that expand the PCjr's capabilities, such as printers, light pens, modems, and joysticks. Special features of the PCjr are highlighted by hands-on tutorials covering graphics and music, and BASIC and Logo. The book also explains how to access information services such as The Source and CompuServe. *Making the Most of the IBM PCjr* will enable you to make home computing one of life's simple pleasures.